Down to Earth
Dressage

**Carl and Donnersong showing off after their 1997
National Prix St Georges Championship win.**

(This great picture captured a moment on Carl's lap of
honour when gentlemen traditionally remove their hats.
The publishers would like to advise that hard hats should
be worn at all times when riding horses.)

HORSE & RIDER

Dedication

For Jannie

who, with Christopher, turned more of what other people considered equine sows' ears into silk purses, than anyone we'll ever know. Thanks for showing there is always a way, that every horse has a talent if we only care to look for it, and for all the laughs.

First published in Great Britain in 1999.
© Bernadette Faurie and Carl Hester

Photos: Steve Bardens, Bob Langrish, David Miller, Kit Houghton, Jo Barry, Albion Saddlemakers, Buxactic

Editor: Alison Bridge
Designer: Jamie Powell
Sub Editors: Sue Beenstock, Sharon Everett

Published by HORSE&RIDER magazine, D J Murphy (Publishers) Ltd, Haslemere House, Lower Street, Haslemere, Surrey GU27 2PE in association with The Kenilworth Press, Addington, Buckingham MK18 2JR.

ISBN 1-872119-20-4

Origination by PPG Ltd, Hilsea, Portsmouth. Printed by Headley Brothers, The Invicta Press, Ashford, Kent.

Acknowledgements: Many thanks to Alison and the D J Murphy team for their huge support, enthusiasm, and hard work in putting our book together - BF & CH.

The Authors

Carl Hester

Born on the tiny, car-less Channel Island of Sark, Carl's early exploits driving tourist carriages and riding bareback are well documented. Heading to the mainland aged 16 to study for his BHSAI, it wasn't long before the naturally competitive Carl began notching up wins in dressage and junior eventing.

The National Young Rider Dressage Championship in 1985, on a skewbald mare named Jolly Dolly, was his first national title. It didn't immediately open doors and after a 'what am I doing' sojourn back on Sark, Carl answered an ad for a live-in person to help with young event and dressage horses.

The following years with Jannie and Christopher Taylor in the Cotswolds were to prove the foundation for his philosophy of training horses.

A big break, employment as rider to Dr and Mrs Bechtolsheimer's stable, led to Carl's team debut at the 1990 World Games in Stockholm on Rubelit von Unkenruf. Then, he was the youngest rider to make a British dressage team. Two years later he was Britain's highest placed dressage rider, 16th, at the Barcelona Olympics on Giorgione.

Carl spread his wings and set up his own training base at Kate Carter's Cotswold yard in 1993. Since then, his tally of national championships has risen to a total of 17. Carl returned to the British team in 1997 for the European championships on Legal Democrat, with whom he has won two of his three national grand prix titles. Carl met the horse and his owner Marcia Kelsey, when they came for lessons as winners of **HORSE&RIDER** magazine's 'Search for a Star'.

Bernadette Faurie

Bernie started riding at the age of eight with fortnightly lessons snatched in the school lunch hour, aided and abetted by her mother, who gave in after Bernie had worn out successive pairs of ballet shoes cantering round the garden.

The horse-mad kid's time-honoured route to riding, working in return for training, produced lots of opportunities for Bernie as Marjorie Ramsey had the knack of spotting future show and jumping ponies from under woolly coverings. During several London-based years working in advertising, horses took a back seat, but when the lure proved too strong, Bernie became a horse owner for the first time.

'Massey', as a learning curve, was 10 horses rolled into one. Show jumping, eventing and later dressage, she did it all, sometimes brilliantly, sometimes exasperatingly. Through Massey, Bernie moved to the Cotswolds, meeting Carl when he evented for the Taylors, and another important friend, Miranda Morley, whose suggestion that Bernie wrote a report on her show was the catalyst for a major change. Three months later, writing, formerly a minor part of the programme, was a full-time job.

Bernadette Faurie is a chief correspondent for *Horse International* and contributes to several major equestrian titles, including, of course, **HORSE&RIDER** magazine. In 1996, she was voted 'Dressage Journalist of the Year' by the International Trainers Club. She has also written on a variety of subjects from fashion to football and is the Editor of a transnational security and crime journal.

Contents

Section 1

Perfect Paces

Introduction

What is dressage?

For some it's a passion, but for others it's a series of complex mysteries, inaccessible to the uninitiated, or at least something to get over with as soon as possible.

Dressage is an art, it's a sport, but the bottom line is, it's training. Even the word 'dressage' is derived from the French verb 'dresser' meaning, for animals, 'to train'.

Forget the misconception that dressage is all about movements, even 'tricks'. Call it flat work, call it dressage, 'it' is essential training for a horse to be successful in any sphere.

Everyone who rides has some contact with dressage as a basic training strategy for horse and rider that not only makes riding more pleasurable, but also safer. To be able to stop to let a car past on a hack requires basic training.

The show jumper who wins against the clock does it because his horse is quicker off the rider's aids, more supple to make tighter turns and can lengthen or shorten his stride more easily to cope with different distances.

The event horse that can take on bounces at an angle or the narrowest arrowhead with complete accuracy can do so because he is trained to be gymnastic, and listen to his rider.

Then of course there is the dressage horse. Dressage at its best looks beautiful, harmonious and artistic. Watch the top combinations in the freestyle at World, European and Olympic Championships.

To make the grade at that level doesn't just require a talented rider, dedication and concentration, you need an exceptionally talented horse and many very good riders meet only one star in their lifetime.

Whereas not everyone who goes jogging thinks they have to make the next Olympics, a lot of people are too hard on themselves or their horses when it comes to dressage. Not everybody is going to make the Olympics, or even grand prix, and even if you have a horse with brilliant paces, it's a long road not everyone can reach the end of, and it takes talent, training, patience and often a large portion of luck as well.

If your horse doesn't have the most brilliant movement, or gets a bit fizzy perhaps, that's no reason to stop you making the best out of what you've got, and why stop at novice? Throughout this book, we are talking about training and movements that any horse can do with the right groundwork.

OK, you might think, Carl's been to the Olympics (and hopefully will again) and has a stable of talented horses to train. True, but there has been a lot of hard work and ups and downs along the way and, in horse terms, many sows' ears until the potential silk purses started to arrive. Then, as you'll see throughout the book, even 'purpose-built' horses aren't perfect, and they are never machines.

That's why we are saying you and your horse can 'do dressage', whether you want to compete happily at riding club competitions and feel safer on hacks, or jump faster clear rounds, go advanced eventing, or get as far as you can in dressage.

This book aims to set out the basic components you need to make a horse more pleasing to ride and more athletic in his body, which in turn will keep him healthier as more capable of maximising his potential. We also aim to make it enjoyable for every rider to make the most of his or her own potential.

That's the real key word, enjoyment. Whether you ride as a hobby or spend your life riding as a professional, you've got to be able to have a laugh while you're doing it.

We're not saying it's easy or that there won't be moments of frustration. There will be. But, there'll be plenty of 'highs' and a real sense of achievement as well. That's all part and parcel of doing any job well.

Just bear in mind that while it might be dressage, it's got to be fun.

Introduction

Carl, Bernie and horses

A word from Carl

I'd just like to say how much I enjoying doing this book with Bernie. Other people might do things differently, and what we've said here is based only on what I've experienced.

First and foremost, I love my horses and want the best lives possible for them. I think the most important thing for you to keep in mind is, to get the best from horses, you have to listen to them.

I'd like to think I do things along classical lines, but a horse's personality and conformation, which can be very different, also play a big part in training - as you can see by the different shapes and sizes of the horses you'll meet in this book.

As may be with some of yours, not all of my horses will necessarily make grand prix, but I'm having great fun learning from them, and training them as far as they can go.

While putting this book together, looking through the many photographs, I realised how far there is still to go to. My position, the horses' way of going, it could be better! That's the reason to always keep improving.

A word from Bernie

In the whole time I've known Carl, I've never once known him blame a horse when something is not going right. We're all human, and so is Carl, but what is special about him as a rider is that first and foremost, he's a horseman.

He loves his horses, they love him and they trust him because as much as he nurtures their talent, he also knows their limitations. Every horse can be himself.

I'm the first to admit that the word 'dressage' used to induce the same effect on me as maths at school - instant narcolepsy. Flatwork though, was OK. I was very lucky, as a kid, to have learned basic correct riding, but scaring myself silly over fences seemed much more fun than going round in circles.

What changed? Learning that dressage was nothing to do with going round in circles, and Carl had a lot to do with that. Perhaps even more momentously, he had a lot to do with making it fun.

Carl's horses

Donnersong

'Otto' to his friends, was homebred by his owners, Kate Carter and her mother Pat Masek. He is by Karin Rehbein's German team horse Donnerhall out of Pastiche, an Oldenburg mare by Pik Trumf.

Once he'd actually allowed a rider to get on and stay on, it was clear Otto had talent. He loved the limelight right from the start of his competitive career, winning the National Advanced Medium championship in his first season as a six-year-old.

Carl, together with Otto's connections and considerable fan club, was thrilled when he took the Prix St Georges Championship as a seven-year-old, followed early the next year by the small tour championship at the prestigious Zwolle Stallion show in Holland.

It's a big step from small tour to grand prix, probably the biggest step in the dressage horse's career, so concentration on that ultimate aim has been the main goal for Otto.

He also has stud duties to consider. Approved by the Anglo European Studbook and the Sport Horse Breeding of Great Britain, Otto's first foals were born in 1998.

Donner Rhapsody

'Madonna' at home, is Donnersong's full sister, two years younger. In this book she is our model - and in her outlook she's very much the supermodel - for the vital four to six-year-old training years.

Madonna made a successful debut to the competitive scene, winning two novices and one elementary class ridden by her owner Kate Carter. Carl then took over the ride for Madonna's medium season. While Kate was intending to take over when she was less busy with her twin boys, Carl was having so much fun with Madonna, she realised this would be no easy task!

Fantastic Elastic

Carl picked Elastic out of a bunch of wild young two-year-olds in Holland. Why him? He was timid and unhandled, but definitely had personality as well as loose paces.

By Clavecimbel, breeder Bert Rutten's international stallion, Elastic was so big as a baby horse he spent his first couple of years under saddle hacking and growing up. Again, he was not the easiest to back, in fact Carl's description on this one is not suitable for family viewing!

When he started to mature, however, it was into quite a star. He was second in the Winter Novice Championships as a five-year-old, with Spencer Wilton riding as Carl is not eligible to ride at that level. The next year, watched proudly by owners Paul and Carol Christie, he and Carl won Britain's richest dressage prize, the Equilibra Challenge, with a mark of 9.75 out of 10.

Elastic proved extremely talented for grand prix work very quickly, but he had to wait until he was mature enough in his mind to go on to the higher levels, so Carl let Spencer ride him for a season to settle him at shows. As he was rather exuberant on outings, this meant working through it and not getting depressed about any low scores.

On the strength of Elastic's personality and talent, Carl bought his full brother.

Hot Shot

Known as 'Brad', Hot Shot is our model for the four-year-old 'baby' stages of a horse's schooling.

Carl bought him in Holland as a two-year-old too, attracted by his elegance and beautiful head and neck. Holstein bred by Accord II, Brad's a very different type from Elastic and has many more Thoroughbred characteristics about him.

After being started at his basic lessons, Brad spent a good few months just hacking and playing before starting real school.

Maxwel

Bred in Denmark, Maxwel brought a lot of joy to his owner Roly Luard, and of course Carl, when he won both the national Prix St Georges and Intermediaire Championships in 1998.

The following year he was sold to Carl's pupil Gemma Green, who was looking forward to gaining loads of valuable experience and fun at junior and young rider levels with Maxwel.

Perfect Paces

The paces or gaits, together with the transitions, the changes between or within the paces, are your tools for establishing good basic training.

You may think any horse can already perform walk, trot and canter and change between each pace perfectly well. So he can, in the field, but put a rider on his back and his whole balance changes. The ridden horse needs to relearn how to carry himself with lightness and ease, and the rider needs to learn how to help him.

The quality of any horse's natural paces can be improved. Work at perfecting the paces, and not only will you go a long way towards impressing a dressage judge, but also find your horse a real pleasure to ride. This is where down to earth dressage training starts.

Chapter one

The Walk

Training a horse for dressage is a long process of developing more lightness and expression in the horse's natural movements. The basic gaits are your raw materials: walk, trot and canter.

Of the three, the walk is often the one given least attention but this is a big mistake. First off, a flashy trot or a big canter has turned the head of many a horse buyer who gets their prospective Olympic medallist home to find he's got the walk of a llama.

In training, walk is the hardest pace to improve and the easiest to ruin. But you're going to need to preserve and improve your horse's walk if you want to get anywhere on the road from novice to grand prix level.

Back to basics

So what is a good walk? Your horse should put his feet down in a clear four-beat rhythm, with equal weight on every beat. A ballet teacher would count the time as, 'one and two and three and four and...'.

You can hear an incorrect walk before you see it. It is either hurried into a onetwothreefour, or unequal rhythm between the beats, or, horror of horrors, a mere one-two. It is, in fact, very, very rare, if not impossible, to find a horse with a naturally

Madonna at four showing off her wonderfully free walk: 'It's a cool, loose sashay that is a real gem in a novice test - you'd be mad to play around with it,' says Carl.

incorrect walk, one that paces in diagonal pairs or near enough.

However, some horses will have a shorter walk than others and it's usually tense horses, those who naturally do not move with looseness in the shoulder, or who do not step under as actively as they should from behind. But don't worry - all these things can be improved.

Do not disturb!

The key factor with the walk is not to disturb it in the first place. With a young horse, such as Madonna when she was five and getting her first glimpse of the big wide world in novice competition, walking on the bit had not even featured in her repertoire.

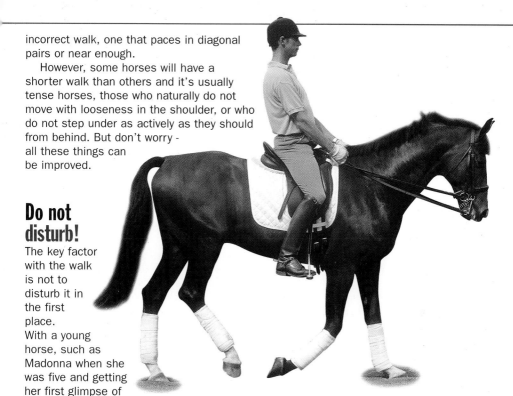

It might surprise some people, because at novice level the requirements for medium walk ask for the horse to remain on the bit. However, Carl prefers to look at it as maintaining a soft, steady contact. The reason is simple. By imagining that you're pushing the horse's head and neck away, the frame and the steps lengthen. If you get hold of the front end and then push, the steps get shorter as there is nowhere for the momentum to go.

You often see a novice rider in a test at walk working hard with their legs and body but the horse is not responding. If they have to work so hard to get the horse to keep going forward in walk, how are they going to get him to do anything else?

And then there are the people you see, even out hacking, thinking of the outline first, the 'I've got to keep his head in,' syndrome. They have fiddled the horse's head down and in their desire to keep him there, let the action of the horse's legs stack up rather than allowing the sequence to move him forward, so it becomes an incorrect sequence.

The big difference with walk is that there is neither the suspension nor the impulsion of the other paces to play with, which is why trying to fix problems from the front end has such dire consequences. So this is why it's essential not to tamper with the horse's walk. Start by moving forwards with a soft steady contact. But if you do have problems or want to improve, read on.

Otto in medium walk; the horse should be marching freely with regular, unrestricted, energetic strides.

The different walks

In extended walk, Otto clearly overtracks, covering masses of ground, while Carl allows his neck and head to stretch.

Basic walks

In the basic stages (ie preliminary and novice level in competition) you need to be able to produce medium walk and free walk on a long rein.

Medium walk

In this basic walk the horse should be freely marching forwards with regular, unrestricted and energetic strides.

● The hind feet should touch the ground in front of the prints of the fore feet, which is known as overtracking.
● The rider maintains a steady and sympathetic contact which allows the horse's head and neck to move with the stride, much more than in trot or canter.

Free walk on a long rein

This walk is all about relaxation. The horse has complete freedom to lower and stretch his head and neck. One thing to remember is that it is a long, but not a loose, rein.

● When riding the movement, which is usually asked for on a diagonal, get onto your line then gradually and smoothly let the reins go to accommodate the stretch in the neck.

● The horse mustn't snatch the reins. If he does it is probably because he has been restricted by the rider's hands in the preceding movements, and by snatching he's just announced the fact to the judge.

● Don't chuck the reins at the horse suddenly, he'll pop his head up and look around to find out where you've gone.

More advanced walks

Extended walk

Introduced in competitions from elementary upwards.

● Without quickening the beat, and without losing the regular rhythm, the horse should cover as much ground as he can, with a very clear over-track.

● The rider allows the stretch of the head and neck while keeping a soft contact on the horse's mouth.

Collected walk

Introduced at elementary level, the collected walk should show the clear, four-beat, forward rhythm.

● Having developed self-carriage and engagement, the horse should be able to show higher, more cadenced and less ground-covering steps in collected walk because the bending of the joints is more pronounced and there is more contained activity.

● The increased self-carriage means the horse carries his head and neck proudly and lightly.

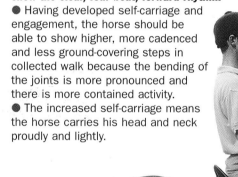

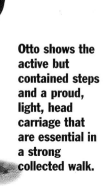

Otto shows the active but contained steps and a proud, light, head carriage that are essential in a strong collected walk.

Walk homework

Working at home, ideally you'll give the horse a good 10 minutes walking to loosen up before you start schooling work. But if the horse is feeling particularly cheeky or tense, move into trot and settle him rather than insisting on a calm walk that isn't going to happen and is only going to end up marring the pace.

Carry on the good work on walk outside the school. Carl

Elastic relaxes into free walk on a loose rein. The move is all about stretching, not grabbing the rider's hands.

Free walk on a loose rein

This is not asked for as a test movement, but at the end of a working session, there is nothing more satisfying for both rider and horse than when, for the final cooling-off period, the rider can completely give the reins and the horse marches actively, stretching his head and neck, thoroughly relaxed.

hacks all his horses at least once a week, and most days they all have a relaxed walk round the field after their schooling sessions. Not only does this help them mentally, but a happy horse marching out on a long rein is developing his walk for himself.

One thing that really helps improve a walk is walking up and down hills. The horse has to push more from behind and as a result he will naturally lower and stretch his neck.

Carl's horses

Otto

Carl did a lot of hill work work with Otto, a stallion with an 'I'm-king-of-the-castle' attitude, which tended to make him inattentive at walk. He'd either be in a hurry to do something more interesting and tighten his steps or jog, or be so busy surveying his kingdom while announcing his presence to his fans that getting him to stretch was a major feat.

Madonna

With Madonna, his younger sister, it was a different matter. She is more the catwalk model type, an equine Claudia Schiffer who shows off with a cool, loose sashay which proved to be a real gem in a novice test. At that stage, you'd be mad to play around with it.

Elastic

Elastic has an excellent free walk, but he tended to tense when walking 'on the bit', so most of his walk work was done on a long rein, to make sure tension was not allowed to spoil the quality of the pace. Using some lateral work in walk, a little leg-yield and shoulder-in, helped to relax Elastic's walk.

Laziness

The horse should walk under his own steam, without constant encouragement from the rider. In other words, he should be in front of the leg.

What to do

If he is a bit lazy, you need to give one sharp kick with the legs to wake him up, making sure you don't block it with your hands. Once he's responded, you can be lighter with your aids.

Irregular footfalls

Shoulder-in (see Chapter 9) is the single best secret weapon in helping to improve the walk.

What to do

If the horse has a faulty sequence in walk, by riding him in a correct shoulder-in he has to engage his inside leg and step under, which improves the pace immediately.

Sharp horses

With a sharp horse that has the tendency to run away from the leg in walk, shoulder-in is also a good exercise in that it has the advantage of teaching the horse to accept the rider's leg.

What to do

The horse has to accept your leg, even if he walks for himself, because you have to keep him straight and direct the line you want him to take.

Stiff neck

Sometimes you need to mobilise and free the horse's head and neck by bending before the horse will willingly stretch himself.

What to do

This is where the shoulder-in bend helps. Once the horse is offering to stretch, whatever you do don't pull down on the bit. Instead, encourage the stretch to happen by following it forwards with your hands.

Jogging

In a test, the walk is often an excuse for a break in concentration or anticipation.

What to do

One thing to practise at home is to ride a 10m circle before your diagonal of free walk and then another at the end of the diagonal. This tends to encourage the horse to listen and wait, rather than anticipate and run. It also helps the rider to keep the lower leg on, which in turn helps to prevent the horse breaking into a jog at the end.

Chapter two

The Trot

If you think the trot is a big chance to show off, you're right! An extended trot which sets off as if the horse is climbing like Concorde on take-off, and powers across the diagonal with the lift and expression of a Nureyev, is a real attention grabber. There's one problem: it's only part of the trot story and it's not that easy! The good news is that, of all the paces, the trot is the one you can work miracles on. Here's how you do it.

Back to basics

The rhythm of the trot is two-time, as the horse's legs move in alternate diagonal pairs, with a moment of suspension in between. You can't really break the two-time sequence, otherwise you'd be doing something other than trotting. But you can lose the regularity and, in Carl's opinion, and that of all good judges, irregularity breeds contempt and is to be avoided at all costs.

A horse's basic trot style varies according to his conformation, type and breeding. What it should always be, however, is free, active, regular, balanced, rhythmic and swinging.

Madonna at four years old in a nice, forward, working trot.

What to avoid

In the quest for the 'get noticed' big trot, you'll see riders head off at 90 miles an hour flat out with the horse stuck rigidly on the hand. The rider is usually sitting behind the vertical and pushing as if about to give birth.

All this style of riding does is to push the hindlegs out and the back away, when what you actually need for lots of expression in trot is a high degree of suppleness, muscular development and engagement. In other words, before you can ask

Basic trots

The basic trot is working trot. In competition, at preliminary and novice level, tests ask for working trot and also for a few lengthened strides.

for full power in extension, you've got to be able to collect.

The other common mistake in trying to get a big trot is to over-ride and cling on to the moment of suspension, creating a passage-like impression. That's also a no-no in the suppleness stakes, and when you want to make transitions into and within the pace you'll be stuck, not to mention the problems you'll have when you really do want to ask for passage.

Working trot

Working trot is all about balance and impulsion. The horse should work forward with even, elastic steps coming from active hindlegs and flexing hocks over a supple back to a soft, steady contact on the bit.

Showing a few lengthened strides

In a test, the judge wants to see rudiments of correct training towards medium trot, the ability of the horse to lengthen his stride and frame while keeping his impulsion, balance and rhythm into the basic lengthening and back again into working trot.

Slowing the trot (above) and a few lengthened strides (below).

Medium trot

Again, medium trot first appears at elementary level. On the trot scale, medium is between working and extended trot.

● With obvious impulsion from behind, the horse makes a clear, even and balanced lengthening of his steps.

● He should keep the same rhythm and remain steadily on the bit.

● The rider should allow the horse to lower his head and neck slightly to accommodate the lengthening of his frame.

More advanced trots

Collected trot

This trot starts to appear on the test sheets at elementary level, which unfortunately too often has the effect of producing elementary horses who have lost their forward momentum. The rider uses the hand to fake it rather than waiting until the horse is sufficiently trained to take more weight on his hindquarters.

● In a genuine collected trot, rhythm has developed into cadence.

● The increased level of engagement and impulsion is contained in lightness and self carriage, with the shoulder free and the neck arched on to the bit.

● The steps are shorter than in the other trots, but very light and mobile and equally expressive on the straight and in lateral work.

Extended trot

This is maximum power from maximum impulsion. In a really super extended trot, the picture will look almost as if the horse is not touching the ground.

● The horse should keep the same rhythm and tempo while covering as much ground as possible.

Madonna at six in medium trot, top. You can see clearly how her trot has improved between this and the photos on the left when she was four. Now she has more engagement, balance, power from the quarters and a great deal more confidence.

Otto in collected trot, above.

● He'll lengthen and lower his frame, but mustn't end up leaning on the bit as he gains ground.

● The forefoot should land in the spot to which it is pointing, while in a freeze frame, the hindleg will appear to be coming halfway or more underneath the horse's tummy.

● The fore and hindlegs should match, but when you get a horse able to reach incredibly high with his forelegs, as long as the hindlegs are doing the maximum, the judges should love it. Carl used to get very miffed when one judge only gave Giorgione (who was extra-expressive in front in his heyday) a five for extended trot. But, if he'd have done with his hindlegs what he did in front, he'd have ended up with a very sore tummy.

Improving the trot

The best way to develop the trot is through transitions, and Carl doesn't mean the odd one as a change from going round in circles but lots of them.

Canter-trot-trot-canter

The best way to encourage swing is by using canter-trot-trot-canter which activates the hindlegs, getting the horse to push more from the hocks and take more weight on his back end.

On and back

The basic transition within the pace is invaluable too. Carl calls it 'on and back', as it's basically a few lengthened

Elastic shows great promise as he lengthens in trot.

strides, then back to normal.

Don't do more 'on' than your horse's balance can cope with at his particular stage in training. A few balanced, rhythmic 'on' steps can be built up, but if you ask too much too soon, the horse will lose his balance and his confidence. If he breaks into canter in the early stages, don't be hard on him as he is offering to go forwards, which is, after all, what you want. Start again and don't ask for so much.

Ride forwards

Remember transitions, including downward ones, must always be ridden forwards if you are going to get any benefit out of this work. When you ask the horse to go on and lengthen, your hands must allow for a lengthened frame, otherwise you'll block the forward movement and send the hindlegs just where you don't want them, out of the back door.

Carl's horses

Otto

To start with, and much to Carl's dismay, Otto had a minuscule trot, as he pulled from the front, rather than pushing from behind. Carl set about teaching him to develop more suspension by using the 'on and back' transition technique (see above) riding the 'back' almost in passage.

The transitions also helped his submission, so he learned to wait as well as taking more weight on his hindlegs. He's a terrible show-off, so now, needless to say, he's rather keen to help Carl develop his trot, including a very promising extension.

When he won the Prix St Georges Championships, Carl purposely went for more correctness than flashiness, because Otto was still only seven and not physically ready for full power. If he had been, Carl would have had nothing left in his arsenal for grand prix level.

Madonna

When Madonna was just starting novice tests at four years old, she had naturally well-engaged hindlegs but she tended to push too much on to her front and needed to learn how to balance herself. If Carl rode her forwards too much, she tended to run too much on the hand, so he concentrated on riding her in a softer, slower trot, so that the hindlegs were waiting and taking more weight.

Elastic

Elastic has a very loose trot, and he is naturally good at passage. That's great, but Carl had to be very careful with this. A lot of forward work in trot, sticking to the working pace so Elastic could develop his strength before exercising this natural ability to collect was essential to avoid him 'hovering' in trot rather than moving truly forward from behind.

Test tactics

● There's nothing that cramps the style of a good trot quicker than a tense rider. You don't have to sit the whole way through the test at preliminary and novice levels, go rising rather than flatten the stride.

● Think of pushing the horse out in front of you.

● Think rhythm all the way. If it helps, keep a favourite tune in your head to relax and keep the rhythmic pace.

● Don't ask for more than you can cope with. A flashy trot is one thing, but you've got to be able to go directly into halt from it.

● With lengthened strides, think gradual. Don't try for a flashy medium trot which is not asked for and risk losing balance. If you do break into canter, keep cool, correct it and ask again. You'll get more points than if you simply give up.

Elastic working 'deep and round' in trot.

'Deep and round'

There is a lot of talk about 'deep and round', but the crucial factor in working this way is that the horse is soft and light even though he is deeper in his outline, works from behind, over his back and neck and lifts from his shoulder.

The objective is to stretch and supple the whole top line so the horse can relax, soften and really start to swing though his back.

Carl always gives his horses a relaxation period in trot and canter, working them in this deeper outline, rising in trot or lightening his seat in canter. It helps develop rhythm and promotes development of the right muscles in the right way.

As the horse relaxes mentally, he is automatically in a position to allow himself to develop his suppleness. It's an integral part of gymnastic training.

The root of trot problems

A good rhythm can't be maintained unless the horse is supple and in balance.

Causes of irregularity in the trot include the following:

Horse
● Stiffness and a loss of balance.

Rider
● Sitting crooked.
● Uneven contact, pulling more on one rein.
● Pushing the horse out of natural stride without impulsion or engagement.

Small trots

Horses with small trots should be ridden in rising trot as much as possible, get your behind out of the saddle so he can learn to use his back and start to swing.

Chapter three

The Canter

Canter is such an exciting pace to work with. Apart from giving you the chance to give free rein to expression in your earlier tests, later on the quality of your pirouettes and changes, which account for so many marks at top level, grand prix, depend entirely on the quality of the canter.

Get a video and watch the Olympic, World and European Champion Isabell Werth and Nobilis Gigolo FRH in their freestyle to music. They produce an extended canter across the diagonal that could worry the best at the Cheltenham Festival and at the end, return to a perfect pirouette without so much as a tweak on the reins from the rider!

Canter in the test means drama and self-expression. What you need to achieve is that expression, but without drama.

Back to basics

The three-time rhythm of the canter, first hindleg, then diagonal pair followed by leading foreleg, should be as clear as a bell, just like a favourite waltz rhythm.

An ideal canter is a bounding stride, coming from a hindleg jumping right underneath the horse's body, which in turn lifts the shoulder producing a light front end. It should look light and easy while being primed with so much contained power that if a 5ft fence popped up at the end of the long side of the school you'd just sail it.

Carl likes to work most of his young horses on a circle in canter so that they don't learn to associate the promise of open space with a chance to get too onward bound and bowl onto the rider's hand. It is much easier to balance a horse if he is in a position to be around the leg and soft in the hand.

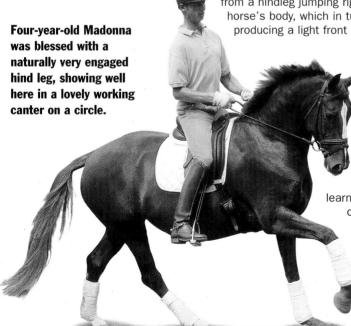

Four-year-old Madonna was blessed with a naturally very engaged hind leg, showing well here in a lovely working canter on a circle.

In medium canter, Otto shows that he can extend well in a self-contained way, above.

Elastic's medium canter shows a good lengthening of his outline, above right.

Why canter might go off the rails

● Collecting too early before the horse has developed enough weight-carrying strength behind. If you shorten the canter, before the hindleg can stay engaged and active enough, it's the quickest recipe for a four-beat, incorrect, canter. You've lost the suspension because the horse isn't strong enough to sustain it, he's had to put his landing gear down to try and keep his balance and the collection is coming from the front end, not the back.

● Strangling the canter by holding the horse back too much. Canter is the most forward pace, the route to speed, so you can understand the nervous rider's tendency to strangle this forward momentum for fear of losing control. But even if your horse is very forward going, it doesn't mean you should take your leg off.

A good contact and keeping your leg on helps to maintain balance. Think about what you're going to do later on. Say you're asking for a flying change every one or two strides; your

leg has to be there to support your request and say to the horse 'stay here' until you signal to swap to the other lead, and vice versa.

Basic canters

Working canter

In this basic canter what's important is the impulsion from the horse's hindlegs, and that it is conveyed freely into a balanced, even, three-time stride, with the horse lightly accepting the contact.

Progressively show some lengthened strides

This movement is designed to show that the horse, while not yet ready to show direct transitions within the pace, is able to lengthen his stride, covering more ground, while retaining his balance and rhythm, and that he will come back to his rider maintaining the same balance and rhythm. 'Progressive' means the rider can use his discretion when to ask for the lengthened strides, and how much.

Test canters

Working canter is what you need for preliminary and novice tests. At novice level you'll be asked to progressively show some lengthened strides, and at elementary level you'll need to show the first degrees of collection and medium canter.

More advanced canters

Otto has the light forehand and engaged hindquarters that you're aiming for in collected canter.

Medium canter

Medium is between working and extended canter and the judge wants to see a free, balanced stride with obvious impulsion and the ability to extend in a self-contained balance, but at a moderate, not full-on level.

The rider should accommodate the horse's reach without restriction while keeping a soft, secure contact. It is nearest to the 'on' that you'll use at home in the 'on and back' work described in this book.

Extended canter

This is the full-on canter, go for broke when you dare, but only when your horse is ready. That is the catchphrase, because the rhythm, tempo and balance must be maintained, as must calmness and lightness. The horse will still be on the bit but the rider allows the horse to reach and stretch his head and neck as he produces, ultimately, the maximum ground-covering strides.

Collected canter

The horse in collected canter has reached a high degree of balance and self-carriage. His hindquarters have developed the power and strength to carry his weight so that his shoulders and forehand are free and light, as is the rider's contact.

Obviously, this amount of development comes in stages. What you can expect at medium level and grand prix are very different degrees of development, a point to bear in mind throughout training. Also remember that slower doesn't equal collection, especially if it is done from the front of the horse.

If you think of the degrees of collection as a graduated increase in cadence, in other words a more defined moment of suspension, achieved through increased strength and balance rather than a shortened stride, then you won't go far wrong.

Getting the best out of canter

Your best secret weapons for improving a canter are shoulder-in and counter canter, combined with the 'on and back' work we've focussed on through this book.

Shoulder-in

Ride shoulder-in in canter to increase the horse's flexibility and engagement (see Chapter 9, Shoulder-in).

If the shoulder-in is ridden truly, not just as neck bend, the horse's inside hind steps under more, taking more weight, so the shoulder becomes more mobile and the forehand lightens.

Counter canter

Counter canter (with the outside leg leading) is especially brilliant for improving the canter. Build it up until you can ride a big circle in counter canter.

The thing to remember is that at home you can ride for athletic development, not just the movements you do in a test. So, for example, if you ride a right hand circle in canter left, you can ask for bend to the right. This gives the horse's left side a stretch workout as he has to use his left hindleg more. It all helps to engage and strengthen the stride from behind which is what we want to work on - and keep working on right up to grand prix.

Canter-halt-canter

Canter-halt-canter on a circle is another gem, especially in improving the long, heavy kind of canter.

Even if you can't do an immediate halt, just stop as soon as the horse is physically capable. Then stand him square, put him on the bit, lighten the rein and strike off. It won't be perfect for a while but the exercise is still doing its job.

The fact that you keep stopping, making the horse round and balanced in halt, then go on, encourages the horse to understand what you want. If you are 'water ski-ing off his back teeth' - Carl's colloquialism for too much weight in the hand - all that will happen is the horse will pull more onto his shoulder and so he won't have a chance to get his hindlegs under. So, try to keep the contact light.

'On and back'

The basic 'on and back' transition within canter is invaluable, too - basically a few lengthened strides, then back to normal.

Don't do more 'on' than the horse's balance can cope with at the stage he is at. A few balanced, rhythmic 'on' steps can be built up, but if you ask too much too soon, the horse will lose his balance and his confidence.

Canter homework

The best way of producing a good canter is not to keep cantering. Transitions are the key to improving paces, plus a few secret schooling weapons.

Carl's horses

Otto

Otto has an exceptional canter, world class. He uses his whole body when he canters. He moves with looseness and this tremendous action from behind which produces the lift and expression up from his shoulder. He just happened to be born with this talent and Carl says it's a joy to sit on!

All he has to do is nurture it, which means developing Otto's muscular and athletic strength for collection. What you do with a canter like this is capitalise on it. Like a precociously gifted child, Otto learned all the more exciting stuff in canter, which in turn helped bring on his trot work.

Madonna

With Madonna at four, Carl adopted a more forward seat in transitions to help her balance. It is a lot easier for a young horse if you take your bottom out of the saddle than if you sit too hard on its back in transitions.

Fortunately, Madonna was blessed with a naturally very engaged hindleg. This is great for the canter, but as the energy she created was strong, it tended to make her strong, so it was not her pace that needed improving but her

submission. Through the stop and start routine of plenty of transitions, Madonna began to understand the basis of the half-halt.

Introducing some counter canter on the long sides of the school helped develop her balance and also gave her something to think about. Letting the horse run on in canter does no good at all. It is far more constructive to stay on a large circle until the horse has developed a decent amount of balance to stay in the same rhythm on long sides and diagonals.

Elastic

Elastic is a very big horse and has the canter to match, so what was important here was to wait until he was strong enough physically before asking him to collect more. Lots of canter-walk-canter transitions helped him learn to shorten his canter in balance without losing the quality of the canter.

Ride forwards!

The worst canter fault is the old four-time beat, but 99% of the time it is a rider problem, or it has been caused by a rider in the past strangling the horse in front so causing the back and mouth to stiffen. There might be other symptoms, but there is rarely any other cause!

In such cases the canter needs to be ridden more forwards and usually deeper to encourage the horse to loosen his back and free up the inside hindleg, in conjunction with the exercises described.

Canter test tactics

● Always ride canter 'up hill'. Imagine there is a 4ft fence at the end of the long side, and it will help you automatically put your mind and body into a position where you are asking the horse to collect and 'bounce', without forcing it. Try it and see the difference!
● Use the short side in the test to let the horse move on a bit and show off his lovely profile to the judge - you've got a corner coming up to get everything ready for the next movement.
● Remember to balance the canter before every transition. If you are aiming to trot at 'C', warn the horse in the corner before - he'll do it better if you don't spring it on him!
● As the rider, concentrate and work on absorbing the movement through your body so you don't block what you are asking for (and this applies to all paces). Canter is a very easy pace to sit on when you can do this, so don't ruin all your hard work by sitting against the movement.

Carl working Elastic deep and round in a lovely relaxed canter.

Revising your paces

As described throughout this book, in walk, trot and canter we want to see and produce forward, expressive paces. In canter, that is a big, bounding loose 'jump' that'll be a joy to any judge's eye.

With all the paces, bear in mind that capitalising on your horse's best pace will reap rewards in the others. Then, the quality of the pace determines the quality of the movement.

It all combines to determine the quality of the test - and your horse's ridden performance in all spheres.

Chapter four

Transitions

Transition is probably the most important word in dressage training. Apart from the fact that you can't even move off without one, transitions are the building blocks you'll need to get the horse from one stage to the next in his development.

As we have stressed so far, transitions are the main tool for developing super gaits. They are also a way of getting the attention of your horse, from a submission and obedience point of view. Ridden in quick succession, transitions get a horse thinking.

The basics

There are two types of transition:
● Changing the gait upwards and downwards.
● Making a difference within the gait.

A perfect transition should look seamless. With an experienced horse it should happen 'just like that', without any hint of abruptness, and at the prescribed marker in a test, which is always when the rider's shoulder is level with the marker.

The cadence of the pace should be maintained right up to and into the new pace or until the moment when the horse halts. All the time, the horse should remain light, calm and maintain his balance and carriage. The rider, meanwhile, should appear to be doing very little.

Preliminary and novice levels

At novice level, transitions to lengthened strides can be progressive, rather than direct. The judge would rather see the rider ask for, and get, a few quality steps, rather than risk pushing the horse out of balance and onto the forehand because at this stage he does not yet have the degree of balance and carriage to make the transition directly.

Walk to canter transitions can also be progressive in some novice tests (check your test sheet) for the same reason: the horse is not, at this stage, expected to be capable of carrying enough weight on the hindquarters to push off directly into canter.

At preliminary and in some novice level tests, you don't have to halt at the beginning, only at the conclusion of your test, which is one less thing to worry about.

Elementary

At elementary level, you'll be asked to show the beginnings of collection, to make all your transitions directly and to show more distinct differences within the paces.

Carl always thinks of collection as an ongoing process of development, rather than an ingredient you suddenly need to add at a certain level. The ability of a young horse to come on and back from a slower trot to a more forward trot at a basic level involves the first degrees of collection.

Medium and upwards

At each level from here on up, the transitions should become increasingly seamless as the horse's balance and carriage develop, until at grand prix he is ready to perform the ultimate in transitions, into piaffe and passage. Even at this top level, the novice grand prix horse will take time to find his balance in getting from the highly cadenced and collected slow 'trot' of passage, to the perfect balance of a sitting piaffe and out again, especially if he is really talented for sitting in piaffe and has a big, expressive passage.

This just goes to show that the work of developing balance and collection through transitions is never finished. It begins as soon as the horse first carries a rider and continues throughout his life.

Tackling transitions

It's a fallacy to think that, once your horse is established in a super trot or canter, the rider's job is to sit there and look pretty. OK, the idea is that you should look pretty and everything should look effortless, but if you think about it logically, at any point in the school (or even on a hack) you'll be approaching or going away from a corner, turn or circle and that is going to involve preparation. Just as free-wheeling in a car gives you no control over manoeuvring, so it is on a horse, you always need to be in the right gear.

Balancing the pace

The most important thing is to get the pace balanced before asking for the transition. It is no good, in a trot-to-halt transition, for example, asking your horse to halt from a very forward trot. An element of collection beforehand gives the hindlegs time to come underneath the horse.

To achieve this, use a half-halt that lasts a stride (see Tools for Transitions, overleaf). If you hold his mouth, the horse will automatically hold your hands. It would be as if you were to keep your foot on the brake while changing gear in the car. Once you apply the horse's brake you're preventing the hindlegs from stepping under him. In both situations you're in danger of skidding.

Tools for transitions

The half-halt

The half-halt is a signal to the horse that something is going to happen. It is almost a gentle restraint, while retaining the power from behind, to get the horse to sit and collect rather than pull forward.

The half-halt lasts for just a stride, don't hold it for four, which is a common debilitating factor in a transition. In itself, the half-halt has a collecting, or gathering, effect. It is almost like your gear change in preparation for the full transition. Here are the three tools which together equal half-halt.

1 The leg

Your leg is only effective if the horse knows what it means. The horse should be sharp off a light leg aid, but he only can be if he understands that leg on means forwards, so that the rest of the time, the rider's leg should be relaxed and just there, rather than clamped round the horse's sides or nagging him at every stride.

2 The seat

A soft seat moves with the horse, allowing his back to breathe under the rider. When a rider that goes with the flow sits a bit deeper, the horse will recognise it as a signal to sit and wait.

3 The hands

A soft contact with forward-thinking fingers allows the horse to carry himself and not lean on the rider's hand or run away from it. When the horse feels a gentle restraint on the rein, he reacts by adjusting his weight and sitting back.

Go for 100 transitions

In schooling sessions, don't think you just need to do a few transitions and then give up. If you tell yourself to do 100 transitions in one session you'll be amazed how quickly you'll have done them. By the end, you'll have a horse that is soft in the rein and waiting for your aids.

Improving response to the rider's leg

A horse that is not in front of the leg in transitions is the sort of horse who needs lots of halt-to-forward transitions. Here's how you do it.

● From halt, on a fairly loose rein so that the head is not clamped down, apply sharp, quick taps with the leg and whip if necessary to send the horse forwards. If the horse breaks into canter, it doesn't matter. Whatever you do, don't punish the horse when he is learning to go forward from your leg. If he canters, he is getting the right idea.

Once the horse has got the idea of moving forwards freely, transitions can be ridden in quick succession to keep the horse thinking.

● The horse that runs away from the leg obviously needs lots of downward transitions. This serves as a useful tool in teaching the horse how to wait for the aid.

Madonna lengthens her stride progressively. At novice level it's better to show just a few quality steps rather than to push the horse out of balance.

Carl's horses

Otto

Otto developed the expression in his trot work through transitions. As a stallion, who knows he's rather wonderful, he tends to think he can go to work while still having a good look round at the talent, so transitions play a major part in reminding him to give his full attention to what he is doing.

As he has a good degree of collection and weight-carrying ability, canter-halt-canter transitions are well within his scope, and a big help in improving his concentration and submission.

Elastic

If there's one thing that makes transition work heavenly it's a horse that's lovely in the rein. That's Elastic! He was such a big, gangly horse when just broken in and needed some time just hacking and working on big circles using progressive transitions until he caught up physically. The result of early caution has made a big horse light on his feet and in the contact and very elegant. If he'd been asked too much too soon, he could have ended up a bit like the loo roll advert - very long and very strong!

Hollowing

This is often caused by the horse running onto the hand, or his fear of the hand when too much pressure is applied to the mouth. It is nearly always a rider problem, stemming from not being independent enough in the seat and relying too much on the hand. If a horse's tendency to hollow is not helped by his conformation, be aware that the problem needs time to solve as new muscles have to build up.

What to do

In upward transitions, make sure you soften the hand to allow the horse to move forward. In downward transitions, you still have to soften the hand as soon as the horse has done what you have asked him to, so that he understands this was the right thing to do. Don't forget that a restraining hand needs a supporting leg and seat to back it up.

Rushing in upward transitions

Rushing is usually a symptom of an inexperienced horse, or a rider who applies the leg aids too strongly and abruptly.

What to do

Ask for the transition more tactfully, with the least possible fuss, and resist the temptation to hang on which will only cause the horse to run away from your hand as well as your leg. Bear in mind that young horses who don't yet understand trot to canter need to run a little bit into canter as they are not very balanced.

Losing straightness in canter transitions

This is caused by the rider asking for too much bend before the transition, and/or forgetting to keep the inside leg on as well as putting the outside leg on, to ask for the strike off.

What to do

The bend should be an inclination, not a turn of the horse's head and neck. If you can see any more of the horse's cheek than the corner of his eye, you've got too much bend. Don't forget that the position of the horse's head and neck is achieved by support from the outside rein, not pulling on the inside.

Can't stop

The brakes won't work if you are not in gear. A horse that runs off also lacks confidence and balance.

What to do

Use lots of transitions on a circle, which gives the rider more time to establish control and the horse less time to gather speed. Take care to sit up and don't be tempted to collapse forward or take the leg off.

Won't go

Either the horse is not responding to your leg, or you are not allowing him to respond by holding on to his mouth.

What to do

You've got to establish the horse's respect for your leg and let him go when he understands what you want.

Test tips

● When the test asks for a transition at a certain marker, don't wait until you are at the marker. Three or four strides before, give the horse a half-halt to warn him that something is going to happen.

● If you have a horse who has a tendency to hollow in transitions, or lose attention, make him a little bit deeper, rather than being just on the bit, before asking for the transition.

● The judge should prefer to see a later, soft transition, rather than a hollow one exactly on the marker. The horse will certainly prefer it, it will help to train him and prepare him for more demanding tests in future.

Madonna

Madonna is naturally forward-going with active hindlegs, so plenty of walk-trot-walk and trot-canter-trot transitions, especially on a big circle, played a vital role in teaching her to wait and begin to sit a little, rather than pushing, full steam ahead, onto her forehand.

Elastic in a trot to walk transition - he feels gentle restraint on the reins, adjusts his weight and sits back.

Chapter five

Halt, move off, rein back

Yes, we know halt and move off are of course transitions, but they are such deceptively simple test movements that it's worth taking time to perfect them. In a test, entry, halt and move off are your first chance to make a good impression on the judge. In training, the transitions to and from halt, and of course that backward movement that must be forwards - rein back - are valuable training aids in themselves.

Halt should always be a forward movement. When reducing the pace to halt, the transition should be smooth and flowing, which is only possible when the rider applies the correct back, leg and rein aids together. The horse should arrive gracefully into a square halt.

When starting with a youngster, halting should be a simple message to the horse. At the beginning of training, it should be just stop and start. The aids are simply this: check on the outside rein to stop, give the rein and touch with the leg. This stop-start method eventually develops into the half-halt.

Start in walk

Check on the rein until you achieve a halt. It is better in the beginning to allow the horse to put his head just where he likes, as long as he actually stands still while he is doing it.

Trying to force the horse onto the bit in halt at this early stage will only encourage a hard mouth and stepping back, which is exactly what you don't want.

Although this is about stopping, you should think of allowing the horse time to step into halt. With a horse that doesn't halt four-square, it is better to begin training by developing a progressive transition into halt, allowing the horse a couple of steps of walk so that he gets the idea of moving forward into the halt. As with all transitions, it is the degree that is important for future development.

An advanced horse can come from collected canter into a square halt because he has the correct degree of collection,

or gathered power, to do it. A young horse who has always been given time to bring his hindlegs underneath him, will find a square halt a natural process, because it is part of that progressive development of weight-carrying ability.

Don't drag the horse into halt with your hands. Check, then let go. If he doesn't stop, give another check, then another, until he does stand still, then allow him to stand on a fairly loose rein. If he moves, check again until he stands. Then give him a pat.

Of course, once you have stopped, let your hands soften, but don't chuck the contact away, which is an instant prompter for the horse to have a look round for his friends.

To move off, leave the rein loose, apply the lower leg aid and walk on.

These are the very basics of a young horse's training.

Madonna moves into halt, bringing her quarters underneath her, making this an active halt, rather than a lazy move into a gradual standstill.

What's important about halt?

A correctly executed halt improves the bending of the hindleg joints. Carl regularly uses halts in the warm-up phase to promote suppleness and obedience in all his horses. After six months of general stop-start aids, he expects the horse to be confident enough to start accepting corrections within the halt.

When we move onto the trot-to-halt and canter-to-halt we

allow progressive steps into and out of halt in the beginning as the horse will not be strong enough to be sufficiently engaged to do direct transitions.

How halt helps

Transitions to halt are especially corrective and useful for horses who are strong in the hand. Every time the horse becomes strong against the rein, if you do a transition to halt and then lighten him off the hand, it's amazing how quickly you can achieve lightness.

When someone advises you to do lots of transitions into halt, it's very easy to imagine that 10 to 15 per session will be sufficient. Wrong! Make that about a 100 in a training session, and then we're talking about a useful exercise.

When the horse understands halt, you can introduce the half-halt, it's the same aids but applied to a lesser degree and in a less sustained way. This is used within the paces and you stop the aid the minute the horse responds.

Test tips

● In a test situation, don't enter in too big a trot which will make the halt difficult to perform in a balanced fashion.

● The more highly strung horse is always going to be susceptible to looking around; constant repetition in training will help cure inattentiveness at halt.

● To get a perfect salute, such as the timely and slick salutes perfected by many an international rider, practise at home, don't just think about it at the show.

● To achieve straightness into the halt, think forwards. A common mistake, when you feel your horse going crooked, is to try and put it right by putting your leg back and pushing the horse back on track. You'll only make it worse. Just ride forwards and think straight and that's where you'll go provided the horse is even in the rein and you are using your legs equally. If the horse squiggles into the halt, you're asking too much from the hand.

● Stepping back in front of the judges is a cardinal sin. Apart from being a sign of inattention, more transitions should have established attention beforehand. It is also another common symptom of a too heavy hand and not enough leg.

P R O B L E M   S O L V I N G

Coming in too fast

The horse needs to be collected in his pace to achieve balance into halt. If you come into halt fast and unbalanced, then you are going to rely too much on the hand to achieve the halt. When you use too much hand, the horse's hindleg is unable to step forward. It's like hitting a brick wall and bouncing back. What happens as you hit the brakes? The horse is made to step back as he hits the rider's hands.

What to do

Never forget that the halt is a forward movement. When teaching the horse to stand square, particularly from a trot-halt transition, in the beginning do it progressively as trot-walk-halt so the horse gets the feeling of forwardness.

Halt not square

This is caused by uneven or incorrect rein contact, in other words, too much hand and not enough leg and back.

What to do

Achieving square halts in tests is much more likely if you pay attention to squaring up every time the horse halts. A friend on the ground can easily point out the rogue foot.

How to tell if the horse is square

Don't lean over and check! This bad habit only encourages the horse to move because he feels you shift your weight. It's only when you're sitting centrally in the saddle that you enable the horse to stand square with equal weight on all four legs.

But it is easy to glance down and check whether the

A fantastic halt at X is easily marred by a wobbly move-off, so imagine you're riding down a tunnel. Here, riding Elastic, Carl proves thought-power really works!

horse's shoulders are parallel in front of you when in halt. Once the shoulders are parallel, sit centrally in the saddle and feel which direction you're leaning towards, the horse will feel longer on that side. So, if you are leaning to the right, the horse's right hind is further out behind him than his left hind.

What to do

To correct this, apply your right leg, not forgetting to keep your contact with the left leg as you want the horse to step forward with the hindleg, not out to the side. The main thing in achieving square halts is to be consistent in your training. If you spend all your time working on this, then let it all go when you stop for a chat with your friends who have just arrived in the school, the horse will not understand. Achieving a good halt has to be a habit.

Keep straight

Riding into halt is all about straightness. Carl says he was always told, for test riding, to imagine punching the judge in front of him with the horse's front feet! OK, it won't earn you too many points if you apply it literally, but the principle works wonders in getting you to ride boldly forwards, and forward riding straightens the horse.

Thinking too much about the line you are on will only make you wobble, think of tightrope walkers. One tip that works is to imagine you are riding down a tunnel, the walls help you keep your aids centered and forward. Carl confesses that he doesn't use this technique himself in the ring at competitions because he's too much of a show off to want to blot out the crowd, but it works.

Moving off

When you ask the horse to move off from halt, it is very important that you have kept your leg on in the halt, as if you suddenly apply your leg, you'll shock the horse into an abrupt transition. When we talk about using your back, this doesn't mean, as is commonly seen, a rider leaning back and applying too much weight on the horse's back. Using your back should entail a slight feeling of bracing the back against the movement, a bit like applying the brakes gently, combined with your reins and legs.

Rein back

There is one very important aspect of halt and move off to which so often not enough attention is paid, rein back. Performed correctly, rein back is not only a mark-earning test movement from novice upwards, but a highly effective schooling tool.

What rein back is

The horse should step back straight and calmly in a clear, diagonal and regular two-time rhythm. In early tests, the horse is asked to step back one horse's length, which is three or four steps. In advanced tests, the judge wants to see a specified number of steps. The most advanced rein back movement is the 'schaukel', a back-forward-back-forward sequence.

What rein back is not

Rein back does NOT mean 'drag-back' or 'run-back'.

Carl and Madonna rein back.

How to ride rein back

Before attempting rein back, the horse needs to be standing square and attentive. Move both your legs into position slightly behind the girth equally, to prevent the horse moving sideways, and prepare to lighten the seat slightly so as not to block the backward steps. As you apply your legs, with both reins equal, feel the reins to prevent the forward movement and encourage the horse to step back. The second you feel this happening, ease the pressure to a light contact mode. If you don't, the horse is likely to reverse at a run. To send the horse forwards again, sit a little deeper, then apply the forward aids.

Rein back as a training tool

● Develops and tests a horse's suppleness and submission to the rider's aids.
● Promotes collection, as it makes the hind leg joints work and the hindquarters take more weight.
● Is useful in correcting strong horses or those that lean on the rider's hand.
● Rein back says 'stop and think' to a horse that is strong or running on, if you halt, ask for a few steps back, then move off straight into trot or canter.
● The horse should be lighter for having sat back on his hindquarters, and listening more to your aids. If he gets strong again, repeat the exercise.

A word of warning Don't ask for too many steps back. Rein back is a strenuous exercise which, if abused, can lead to stress and strain. As with all movements, it is only effective if carried out calmly and correctly.

Chapter six

Engagement

No, this is not advice on how to change your marital status. In dressage, schooling, flat work, whatever you want to call it, engagement is one of those terms that really only crops up when it's missing. You can't ever have too much of it, but you'll soon be aware when you haven't got enough of it, as 'lacking engagement' or 'could be more engaged' pop up on your test sheets. The trouble is it doesn't really tell you what engagement is or why you haven't got enough of it.

Engagement is...

If you have the feeling that you are at one with the horse, that he can execute any manoeuvre you ask with ease, and that includes making a super take-off to a fence, you've got it, plus a lot of other components.

That's the main point about engagement, it is a component. In itself it is a component of collection, and engagement has several components itself. In the collective marks section of the test sheet, engagement of the hindquarters, along with desire to move freely forward, elasticity of the horse's steps and suppleness of the back come under the mark for impulsion.

Engagement is not...

Basically, if you're riding with a feeling from the horse of: 'Here's my head, my bottom's coming,' and wiggling down the centre line trying to get all the parts on the same track, your horse is about as engaged as a hermit's telephone.

Power plus balance plus collection

A horse can be going with lots of flash and dash energy but still not be engaged because he is pulling rather than pushing with his hind legs. Power is one thing, but to develop the full weight-carrying capacity of the horse's hind legs you have to develop balance and collection. That is why you see many horses successful at the lower levels, even up to Prix St Georges, that never make it through to grand prix.

By collection, this means the degree of collection required at your level, not the ultimate required for piaffe and passage if you are only at elementary. Even a four-year-old going in balance, with ease and fluency, has a degree of collection.

You can't produce engagement without power. This is where so many riders go wrong. Thinking too much about control in the early stages or with a young horse, they slow down the horse when what you should do is first put in the power (the desire to go forward) then control it through the half-halt. Confused? People often are, which is why the judges could help sometimes at the lower levels by being more specific. 'Lack of engagement' covers a multitude of sins, and if you work on that before you have your components sorted out you'll only end up with resistance. So first of all, let's analyse the components of engagement.

Desire to go forwards

Engagement has nothing to do with speed but you do have to be going freely forwards. With a young horse, this will mean going through a bit of a wobbly feeling, without being tempted to slow the horse down, before the half-halt is established so you can improve the balance and engagement. You also have to be careful not to go too far the other way and push the horse out of balance, which will create similar problems.

Suppleness

Engagement is all about the horse's willingness to take more weight off the front end onto his hindquarters, the component of collection. For him to be able to do that, the horse has to be supple in his back and neck, and in his

Otto lowers his quarters and steps under further with his hind legs: that's engagement!

Madonna aged four, above right - in the far right photo, aged six, she demonstrates how she has become more engaged behind.

hind legs, not only from the point of view of correctness, but also because if you ask for more without suppleness you're asking for trouble. Stiff joints are vulnerable to injury.

Elasticity

This should work hand-in-hand with suppleness. Only if the horse is supple and strong enough in his back and joints can he move fluently. This component also involves balance and the collection that enables the horse to articulate his joints and move rhythmically.

Tools for engagement

First look at yourself

Are you sitting correctly and in a position to give the horse clear signals effectively and at the right time? It is so easy for people to blame it all on the horse but really be strict with yourself. The horse will always react to what the rider does - it's your job to make sure the horse understands what you want.

Is the horse soft on the bit?

When you ask him to go, the engaged horse should transform the extra power into lift, making bigger and bolder steps, and he takes more weight behind and lightens in his shoulders. This can't happen if the horse runs against your hand.

Is he in front of your leg?

Half-halt is the major key to engagement. Via the half-halt, you can gradually develop the horse's ability to go and come back through transitions between and within the paces to develop that weight-carrying ability.

In the beginning, your transitions will be progressive, becoming more direct as all the components for engagement and the horse's strength become more refined. When you've got that, you've got collection.

Exercises for engagement

Transitions

Once you have checked that all your tools are in good working order, transitions will work for you in promoting engagement through creating more desire and confidence in the horse to use the hind leg.

As we've said, this doesn't mean one or two transitions, but hundreds in every schooling session. In promoting more engagement through transitions, what you are doing is showing the horse that once he works from behind and lifts his shoulder, he will be balanced enough to go round that corner or make that circle.

Think all the time about the quality of your transitions. For example, in a downward transition, the horse can only take the weight back onto the hind legs if he is straight. In the upwards transition the horse can only gather himself to go uphill if he is correctly on the rider's contact.

Circles

Riding circles promotes suppleness, weight-carrying ability and, therefore, engagement. Check that the horse is supple in his back, submissive to the bend and forwards from your leg. The smaller the circle, the more the horse will have to step through with the inside hind, creating more engagement, but it can only happen if the horse is supple and in balance.

Lateral work

Shoulder-in (see chapter 9) is a very useful exercise for promoting engagement, as when the inside hind leg steps under the horse, all the hind leg joints are involved in the workout. It is also a great exercise for improving suppleness, straightness and to get the horse even in the contact. Also, the beauty of this exercise is that with the fizzier, more forward-going horse who finds it hard to wait, shoulder-in helps teach acceptance of the leg aid without running away from it.

Practising shoulder-in is a brilliant way of encouraging engagement.

A gradual process

Engagement and the journey to collection is a gradual process. It is through your day-to-day building and maintenance work that progress is made.

A well-trained horse will make it all look so easy, going forwards and back, gliding smoothly from one movement to the next with fluency. That is engagement and it need not be a big mystery. Now, if you have a problem with engagement, you can go back to the components we've described above, work out where the problem lies and solve it. It might not happen overnight but when it does, it's congratulations on a happy engagement.

Summing up engagement

Balanced and forwards, the horse will give you a feeling that he is light in his shoulder and ready to perform the movements he is ready for with ease. If you look at a really lovely extended trot, the hind quarters will lower into the transition, launching, not lurching. It appears the horse is moving uphill. His hind legs will be clearly coming well underneath him, not pushing out, and although his steps cover the ground, it won't look hurried.

If you watch a really engaged horse moving through a corner, you can easily see his inside hind leg step well forwards, over-tracking into the bend. In a really good piaffe the horse can really sit, lowering his quarters and lightening his forehand while maintaining the steps on the spot with rhythm, balance and energy.

Smart Moves

Smart moves - turns, circles and later the lateral work and flying changes we work on in Section 2 - are your tools for building on the work you started in Section 1. Performing these movements effectively will improve your horse's balance, athletic and gymnastic ability, suppleness and ride-ability. It will also improve his concentration and help deal with tension. You'll also find out how to add variety and purpose to your schooling sessions. Smart moves need to be ridden accurately to be effective, too.

Lateral work, where the horse steps sideways as well as forwards, is an integral part of any horse's athletic training. Don't be afraid of it! As long as your horse has achieved a good degree of balance, is confirmed in his contact with the bit and moves forward freely, you can have a go. Provided you approach lateral work by degrees, starting with a few steps of leg-yield and gradually progressing to half-pass, you'll be amazed what progress you can make.

You couldn't try flying changes - why not? Your horse does them in the field. As with any new lesson, your basic preparation has to be right before attempting changes, but down to earth dressage will guide you through.

Chapter seven

Perfect circles and turns

A perfect circle looks smooth, consistent and it flows. As a test movement, it is a barometer of the horse's ability to adjust the bend of his body to the curvature of the line he follows at the indication of his rider, while remaining supple, free of resistance and maintaining a consistent rhythm and tempo. As a training exercise, circles promote and establish suppleness, attention and balance and are a useful means of containing pace.

Tools for circles

When you're riding a circle, try to keep the following ideas in mind:

- The inside rein may indicate the direction of the bend, but the degree of bend is controlled by the outside rein.
- You hear the phrase, 'around the inside leg', well, in order to create bend in the first place the horse needs to be able to accept contact from a forward-pushing inside leg.
- The rider's outside leg is there to control the quarters: too much and the quarters will come in, not enough and the quarters will swing out. But nothing will happen without that vital inside leg. In canter, because the rider's outside leg indicates the canter lead, there is a higher risk that the horse will bring his quarters in on a circle. So in canter it is important to pay attention to using the inside leg as the impulsion maker, leaving the outside leg to play a support role, ensuring the quarters don't swing out.

Madonna on a circle, producing a smooth, even arc from poll to tail.

What is **bend?**

Length or lateral bend means the horse's body is curved in a smooth, even arc from poll to tail in the direction of the bend. It is only correct if the horse is bent no more in the neck than in the rest of his body, and if he is flexed and soft without tilting his head. Every horse will bend more easily to one side than the other. It's the rider's job to even up a horse's natural tendency through systematic gymnastic training.

There have been all kinds of arguments about which bits of the horse's body can and can't bend. But dressage rules don't require contortion, only suppleness. If you watch a horse out in the field on a sunny day when he turns round and energetically scratches his flank, you'll realise that basically, there's no reason to worry about it.

Suppling exercises with Elastic - a way of enhancing the horse's flexibility, not to be confused with shoulder-in (see page 52 for how to ride this exercise).

Achieving perfect bend

Straighten up

It might seem a contradiction in terms, but making the horse straight is the first step in achieving perfect bend. Ninety-nine percent of horses are crooked on the right. The mistake most people make when they're trying to straighten the horse is to push the hindquarters out, when what you should do is bring the shoulders in. Think of the hind end as the base block and realign the shoulders on to the base.

Lungeing can be very helpful in establishing correct circles, as the horse on the lunge has to perform a continuous turn, the amount of bend being determined by the size of the circle.

A useful suppling exercise

If you ride alongside a wall or fence, you should be able to bend the horse to the inside with a loose inside rein without the shoulders coming in. Eventually you should be able to trot in a straight line like this. This is purely a stretching, suppling

It's so important to sit straight into a turn. You have to be above the horse's centre of gravity so you can push him out in front of you through the circle.

exercise to aid flexibility, certainly not a test movement, and is not to be confused with shoulder-in.

Circle symmetry

When you ride a circle you want to recreate the feeling of the horse being on the lunge - the circle is perfect if he is on a good contact because he is on a continuous turn. What this boils down to is riding forwards. If the horse is too heavy in the hand, or not in front of the leg, there is much more chance of him falling in or out as you try to steer him back on course.

If your own sense of symmetry is the problem, try the old classroom technique of drawing circles, tying a pencil to a piece of string and attaching the other end to a drawing pin, but on a bigger scale. Anchor a lunge line at X and walk round marking out a circle. This is easy in a sand school but you'll have to use your ingenuity with other surfaces.

When you ride the shape, concentrate on riding smoothly forwards until the feeling is familiar, and you can repeat it without your circle mark. Turns are always parts of circles.

A corner, ridden on anything less than an advanced horse, is one quarter of a 10m circle. Add this to a turn onto the centre line for a novice horse and you've got half a 10m circle.

Why circles go pear-shaped

Because it takes more effort to turn than go in a straight line, it is very common to see less experienced riders let the energy level drop as they come into a circle or turn, so the horse dawdles round.

It is much easier to achieve a smooth turn if you have momentum behind you, so preparation is the key: have the horse in front of the leg so he'll respond to a half-halt telling him something is going to happen.

To be in a position to co-ordinate your aids and maintain the energy, you have to be above the horse's centre of gravity, so you can push the horse out in front of you through the turn. Leaning in will put you in a wall of death position leading to an ever-decreasing circle. Leaning out will lead to resistance and loss of bend.

If the horse is not working sufficiently into the outside rein, and it can feel a lot stronger in the contact than on a straight line when he is, it is your inside leg that can remedy the situation. Taking a stronger hold on the outside rein will not cure the problem. Once the inside rein has indicated the degree of bend, you must be ready to ease the hand. Hanging on to the inside rein creates stiffness, resistance and tilting.

Test tips

Tests generally ask for any circular movement on one, then the other, rein. The judge wants to see that the horse is equally supple on both reins.

In a preliminary or novice test, for example in a movement such as 'FD half circle right 10m returning to the track at B', the judge wants to see the bend through a smooth turn with the horse maintaining rhythm, balance and the same length of stride, that you can go straight, and that you can change the bend into the turn at B.

The judge will be looking for the same qualities in a serpentine or in a turn at E and then at B.

Later, at elementary level, the degree of bend will increase to 10m circles and, for example, changing the rein through two half-10m circles. At medium, 10m circles in canter or 20m circles in counter canter are introduced.

● The most common mistake when approaching turns is to overshoot, so you bulge out, the judge sees it head on and you miss out on a perfect centre line. Think about preparing a half circle which you'll start as you reach the quarter marker on the long side, look in the direction you are aiming for and when you hit the centre line, ride boldly forwards.

- If your horse is still at the stage of offering much more bend on one rein while tending to be stiffer to the other ask for less bend on the good side so it isn't so glaringly obvious.

- Don't forget accuracy, not just in the shape of your circle but if the test says 'B circle right 20m', start it at B, then your marker points will be in a position to help you and your score will, hopefully, put you in the ribbons.

Not so good! Elastic leans in and 'motors' round the turn.

Carl's horses

Otto

As he became much more advanced, Otto became more even in both hands but he still needed to do a lot of bending work to keep him supple.

You could call this work 'exercise bending', an enhanced flexing of the neck and body around the rider's inside leg. Carl does this with the horse in stretching position. A young horse who has not yet fully established his strength tends to be more relaxed through his whole body and easier to the rein when he is deeper and rounder, rather than when he is higher in the neck.

Madonna

Madonna was always very good to the left, but to the right tended not to accept the outside left rein, so she could go crooked. To cure this, Carl asked her for lots of changes of direction on big serpentines and voltes with opportunities to straighten her in between to establish a more even contact and her own balance and straightness.

As a real novice, Carl only asked her for bigger circles, 20m full circles and 15m half circles, as she had not yet developed the power in her hind legs to balance on smaller ones.

Chapter eight

Leg-yield

I n Carl's experience, leg-yield is the easiest way of teaching the horse to move away from the leg, even though some riders prefer not to use it because it has no place in dressage tests. You can leg-yield not only from the middle of the school to the side, but also along the long side, where it is sometimes known as shoulders-out. Carl's horses leg-yield at walk, trot and canter, including the advanced horses, as a suppling exercise.

Single focus

In leg-yield, you only have to focus on one thing, and so does the horse, and that is the horse moving off the leg. In this way there is less chance of the steps becoming shorter.

When you move on later to half-pass, you want big, expressive, sweeping steps, which the horse has had a chance to develop from the beginning. He can cross his legs in either direction with maximum suppleness and looseness, having developed the confidence to do so in his early first steps of leg-yield.

Carl turns Brad just before the long side, right, then asks for a few steps of leg-yield back to the wall, far right and above right, exploiting the young horse's tendency to hang to the side of the school.

Bending away

Carl finds that this first stage of moving away from the rider's leg is more naturally accepted when the horse is bending away from the direction he is being asked to move to. In, for example, leg-yield to the left, the horse's head and neck will be positioned to the right.

First steps

In the first stage, leg-yield is done at walk. Just a few steps are very easy to try if you turn up from the track a couple of metres from the long side and ask the horse for two or three steps of leg-yield in walk back to the track.

Young horses tend to hang to the sides or walls of the school, so if you capitalise on this they can cross more easily. At this stage, you are merely teaching the horse to move away from your leg.

Your position in leg-yield

To move the horse away from your leg in leg yield, bring it back a little to the sensitive area behind the girth...

...not so far back that you tickle the numnah!

Madonna in leg-yield to the left along the wall - also known as shoulders-out - far right. With his outside leg back a little, Carl asks for movement away from it. He keeps his weight on the inside and positions Madonna's head to the right.

In all lateral work, the rider should, if anything, sit to the inside, never the outside (if we call the inside the direction of the movement and the outside the direction you are coming from). This doesn't mean leaning in, merely putting more weight onto the inside seat bone and into the inside heel to help distribute your weight evenly. This prevents the inside hip from collapsing, another rider fault in lateral work which disturbs the balance and rhythm. Your shoulders and hips should be parallel to the horse's shoulders.

Leg position
Your outside leg should come back a little to the sensitive area behind the girth but never so far back that you make the hind quarters lead the movement - tickling your numnah gets you nowhere. Your inside leg should just hang by the girth, it's a support which, with the outside rein, controls the angle and degree of crossing.

Relax
It is very easy when you are starting something new to tense up because you are trying hard to remember what you should

be doing. The trouble is, tensing up is the worst thing you can do when asking the horse to move sideways. He simply won't be able to move his body if your weight and aids are in the wrong place.

Use your imagination

If you start with a few leg-yield steps in walk, it's uncomplicated for both you and the horse. Say you are out on a hack and the horse strays from the track while you are admiring the scenery, you are jolted back into action when the image of an irate farmer comes to mind, so your outside leg automatically guides the horse back to the track. That's the principle.

Moving sideways

Shoulders leading

When teaching a young horse, try and let the shoulders into the movement first, then the rest will follow. The major mistake here is to make too much bend in the neck, so the horse loses rhythm and balance, falling out through the outside shoulder.

Reinforcing the aids

If you have trouble moving the horse over with the leg aid, back up your signal with a touch from the schooling whip. The tips for lazy horses apply when moving sideways as much as on a straight line, grinding away at the horse with your leg only creates less response and deadens the horse to the rider's signal.

Lots of breaks

Remember how important it is when starting young horses not to over-stress joints. Give lots of breaks, stretching and forwards, in the lesson.

Leg-yield along the wall

Leg-yielding is an excellent athletic exercise in itself for suppleness. Also, if you feel that the outside rein, your key to correct riding, is becoming stiff, or the horse is hollowing to the inside (ie too much bend to the inside), leg-yielding alongside the wall will help redress the balance and bring the contact back into the outside rein.

At six Madonna finds lateral work easier - here she is leg yielding in canter across the school.

Carl's horses
Brad

Brad has a very elegant movement and three correct paces, so all the expression can be developed through his training.

He is a very confident horse, worldly for his age, which made him receptive to his lessons and very sensible on his weekly hacks. As he became sharper and stronger, Carl was careful to keep him relaxed with lots of stretching exercises to stop any tension building up in his body.

Madonna

Lateral work comes very easily to her. It is a common fact that horses built slightly longer in the body find it easier to cross over with more freedom than the shorter-coupled horses.

As Madonna strengthened up, she became much brighter in her outlook, sometimes resulting in a touch of naughtiness, rather like her big brother in his younger days. Carl worked round it, rather than telling Madonna off, as all that exuberance will stand her in good stead later on in her career.

Chapter nine

Shoulder-in

The long-term objective of using shoulder-in is to achieve a higher degree of collection, balance and lightness in the horse. In turn it will improve straightness. It's also a required movement in dressage tests from elementary upwards.

As an exercise to get the horse level in your hands, shoulder-in is super. It might seem a contradiction in terms to say sideways helps straightness, but the whole point of shoulder-in training is to teach the horse to be straighter. Through bending and going straight the horse becomes more supple and takes more weight on the inside hind.

Shoulder-in exercises all three major hind leg joints, so the suppleness and activity produced gives more freedom to the horse's shoulder.

WHAT PACE?

Shoulder-in is a trot exercise. You can get the feel of going sideways using leg-yield in walk, but shoulder-in is best started from a trot with a brisk, active tempo. Without the energy, the exercise won't be of much use, so if your horse is not really forward-thinking, go back a stage to work on this first before starting shoulder-in.

If you have a fizzy, forward-going type, you'll find shoulder-in a great help as it teaches the horse to accept your leg without running away from it. It's not so easy to run sideways.

Shoulder-in in canter is never asked for as a traditional school movement or in a test but Carl does use this as an exercise to help straighten some horses in canter. It helps promote an active inside hind leg that in turn encourages collection.

Starting shoulder-in on a circle

Carl introduces young horses to shoulder-in on a circle: the advantage is that the horse is already bent round the rider's inside leg, so it's easier for him. Here's how it's done.

● On a circle, indicate the direction inwards with the inside rein.

● Your outside rein stops the horse bending too much to the inside and therefore prevents the outside shoulder falling out.

● Your inside leg maintains the bend and encourages the inside hind leg to step well under the horse's body as well as maintaining the forward flow.

Carl and Maxwel in shoulder-in left along the long side of the school, far right.

● Your outside leg supports, to stop the hindquarters falling out. In any lateral work, you should always concentrate on maintaining the same quality, forward, rhythmic trot as on a straight line.

Shoulder-in down the long side

Once you have established these aspects of shoulder-in on the circle, feeling bend, forward momentum, the horse equal in both reins, you can take to the long side.

At first it is easier to prepare for shoulder-in coming directly out of a corner or 10m circle as you can use the bend you already have and continue to flow up the track. Don't try to ride shoulder-in for the whole long side to start off with. Concentrate on a few good steps.

If you feel the horse stiffen, turn him in a 10m circle to re-establish the bend and rhythm. You can do as many 10m circles as you like up the long side. What you don't want is to bash on in shoulder-in hoping to get it right by the end!

Even while you are learning and using the corners, bear in mind there is a start and finish to this movement, and make sure you straighten the horse at the end before reaching the corner.

Way too much neck bend from Madonna!

More advanced shoulder-in

Progressing to more advanced horses, here's a shoulder-in exercise Carl particularly likes.

● Ride a 20m circle, say left, in shoulder-in right, decreasing the circle to about 10m. Then bring the horse's front end round to the inside, changing to shoulder-in left and gradually increasing the circle back out to 20m. This exercise encourages greater activity and suppleness on both reins, without having to change the rein

Much better! Madonna in shoulder-in with Carl's inside rein asking for the inward bend, the outside rein stops her bending too much. His inside leg maintains the bend and outside leg stops the quarters swinging.

The rider

The rider's weight must be shifted onto the inside seat bone, just push down a little more into your inside stirrup. Don't allow your weight to slide to the outside which then collapses the inside hip. Look up the track in the direction you are going, not down between the horse's ears.

Tips

● Always look for the outside foreleg to come down on the inside of the track.
● If you can see the corner of the horse's eye and the corner of his mouth on the inside, this is enough angle.

Test tips

● The start, shoulder-in and finish should be in the same trot throughout, ie the tempo and length of stride should be the same, and the angle should be symmetrical on both reins.
● Make the corner work for you, use it to prepare for the movement.
● Look in the direction you are heading, not at the inside shoulder if you want to keep on track.

P R O B L E M S O L V I N G

How many tracks?

You may have heard the question of whether shoulder-in should be on three or four tracks? Let's just say that neither is incorrect providing the horse is doing the same thing on both reins and that the angle is equal on both reins. What is important is the bend, which should involve the whole body. Neck bend alone is not shoulder-in.

Falling out

The most common fault is the horse falling out through the outside shoulder. Generally this is because the rider uses too much inside rein to get the bend and not enough inside leg to support it, or fails to maintain the contact on the outside rein. The horse that finds it more difficult to accept the right rein is more likely to fall out to the left.

What to do

You can correct this by having a stronger contact with the outside rein to give more support and by asking for less bend.

Don't pay too much attention if anyone suggests that if your horse is stiffer on one side that it's always down to you. It is common knowledge that most horses are more hollow to the right, so most of you will find shoulder-in on the right rein not as easy to perfect.

Pace deteriorates

The horse's steps shorten in shoulder-in, or you lose impulsion.

What to do

Always straighten and ride boldly forwards to refresh the pace before trying again.

Carl's horses

Madonna

Madonna becomes more relaxed when she does lateral work. It helps her let go, rather than holding herself, and it also helps her become more relaxed in the reins.

Maxwel

He finds lateral work very easy and is very expressive in his sideways steps. Carl uses shoulder-in to keep Maxwel supple and light in the hand.

Elastic

Carl gave Elastic very easy lateral exercises until he had learned to trot in the same rhythm both forwards and sideways. Leg-yield across the diagonal and down the long sides was the main work, with a little bit of shoulder-in, in short bursts, taking care to keep the equal rhythm before, during and after the exercise.

Elastic in 'baby' shoulder-in - you can't expect perfect movements right from the start.

Chapter ten

Travers and half-pass

Don't be afraid of travers and half-pass! If you think of these as useful exercises for working on a horse's ability to bend around the rider's inside leg and engage his quarters, it is not as daunting as thinking of them as 'advanced' dressage movements. If you have mastered leg yield and shoulder-in, and your horse is listening to you, crack on. These are exercises that can encourage much more obedience to the rider's leg and rein aids.

Travers

We start with travers, which is generally ridden on a straight line down the long side of the school, so the rider doesn't have to worry about directing the horse across the arena.

In travers, also known as quarters-in, the horse moves into the direction of the bend and his outside hind leg crosses over in front of his inside hind. The inside hind therefore bears more weight as the horse's weight is moved sideways and across.

Lateral work rules

Before you start travers, or any lateral work, your aids must be fully accepted. The horse must be equally supple on both reins because problems such as uneven contact, or the horse not being forward enough, only get worse or more difficult when you start lateral work, which involves a higher degree of collection.

For those who haven't yet learned lateral work, or taught it

Carl puts Madonna into travers. You can clearly see how he is pushing her quarters into the school with his outside leg, and keeping the weight in his inside heel.

to a horse, it is best to start in walk as this will give you a chance to co-ordinate your aids before moving on to trot and canter.

Getting started in travers

The best way to start travers is to ride the corner onto the long side, then ride the horse straight.

● Bring your outside leg slightly behind the girth in a driving position and push the quarters into the school. The horse will then be at an angle.

● Your inside leg should remain near the girth where it can activate the inside hind leg. That, together with an indication from the inside rein, is the route to achieving correct bend.

● The outside rein meanwhile secures the position of the horse's neck and the degree of bend. To achieve correct bend from your horse you must have a secure inside leg for creating that activity.

● At the end of the long side, to finish the travers, straighten the horse before the corner. This should be done in plenty of time so that on reaching the corner the horse is back on track and totally straight.

P R O B L E M   S O L V I N G

Bending the neck too much, bringing quarters in too much. If you do this it will affect the rhythm and the hind leg will not carry enough weight as it will be pushed too much to the inside.

What to do

To control the front, Carl always thinks of the front of the horse's face looking straight down the track and not to the inside.

Back to basics

As your horse becomes more supple it should be possible to do all the lateral movements we have discussed before, including travers, fluently from one movement to the other without changing the rhythm or outline. If you find you are having difficulties with this, remember always to ask less and stick to your basic rules of straightening the horse in between to achieve proper balance and confidence, rather than pressing on when it is clearly not right.

Maxwel in travers. Carl's outside leg pushes the quarters into the school, his inside rein asks for the horse to bend around his inside leg, which also keeps Maxwel's inside leg active; his outside rein maintains the correct bend.

Half-pass across the school is a great movement for suppling the horse's body and controlling an over-eager horse.

Half-pass

Once you have achieved a good travers, and that means establishing it so you can ride it fluently to order on both reins, not just the one good rein, half-pass should not be a problem. In travers the horse is moving parallel to the side of the school, half-pass is simply travers across a diagonal.

Getting started in half-pass

When teaching half-pass, be prepared to allow the quarters to trail slightly as this will help maintain the essential forward flow. In the beginning, use the long diagonal for half-pass. This is a strenuous exercise that needs to be developed slowly. Only when the horse is strong and confident sideways can you make him really parallel and ask for steeper angles.

What's required in competition?

Half-pass is introduced at medium level and most tests only ask for it from the centre line to the side or vice versa to encourage riders to work forwards in their half-passes. At grand prix, at the other end of the scale, half-passes become much steeper. Horses are expected to cross from one side of the school to the other and back. Then there is the zig-zag which involves changing after a measured number of steps from right half-pass to left, and back and forth.

Progress checklist

To assess the progress of your half-pass training, use this checklist.

● Can you maintain your trot in the same forward rhythm sideways and in a straight line?
● Does your horse remain balanced?
● Do you have the correct bend?

Preparing for half-pass across the diagonal.

Half-pass exercises

Weight into the inside heel

We have talked about leg aids and rein position in travers. In half-pass it is also helpful to think of putting your weight more into your inside heel to encourage the horse to step in that direction.

Carl recalls how it helped him feel for a half-pass by being made to lean right over to the inside to see if he could see the outside hind leg crossing over. It helped him to sit into and feel the direction of the movement he was travelling in, instead of tending to sit to the outside, a common rider fault. This exercise helped him understand about using weight as an aid, but he also adds that it felt as if he was going to fall off, so perhaps this is not one to be tried at home without supervision.

Four steps at a time

When you start riding half-pass on your long diagonal lines, it is a good idea to ride four steps to the side then four straight, then four to the side in a sequence. This enables you to keep control of your horse and your own aids and gives you a chance to correct any faults, such as quarters leading, before they become established.

Quarters leading are the result of either too much or too little bend, which is a control and balance problem.

Half-pass-circle-half-pass

Another useful exercise is to do, say, half-pass to the left, followed by a 10m circle right, followed by half-pass right and vice versa. This not only gives you the feeling of staying in control of your horse's balance but also removes any element of anticipation on the horse's part.

Try it in canter

Some people find it easier to ride half-pass in canter because the co-ordination of the aids is already there. A word of warning, if you establish half-pass in trot first with a good rhythm, you can be sure you are doing the job properly. Taking the easy option in canter can lead to the three-time rhythm breaking up if you only concentrate on going sideways and not on the quality of the pace.

Test Tips

Canter half pass across the school (right).

● Always imagine starting your half-pass with a step of shoulder-in first to stop the horse coming through the corner and starting off with his quarters leading.

● Bring your inside shoulder and inside hip back slightly to give a better impression of you moving with your horse in the direction you are travelling, and not against it.

● When you are thinking of trying your first medium test, read through the tests on offer at your chosen competition rather than entering by numbers. You should always do this anyway, but although we have said most tests at this level start you off in half-pass gently, a couple are deceptively difficult and to be avoided until you are confident at medium.

Carl's horses

Madonna

Travers helped improve Madonna's suppleness through her body and gave Carl more chance to control her as this is a naturally collecting movement. It also curbed her habit of always wanting to run on.

Maxwel

Maxwel has a beautiful flow to his lateral work. He scores high marks as he is always able to maintain a steady rhythm through all his trot work, sideways and straight.

Chapter eleven

Flying Changes

Ever wondered about flying changes but felt intimidated by the thought of trying? A flying change happens at the moment of suspension between two canter strides. A lot of horses perform them when free in the field. Here's how to try them when your horse is under saddle.

Be flexible

No way is it possible lay down hard and fast rules on how to teach changes. If we did it would lead to mechanical, rather than expressive changes, which is the last thing you want. It is up to the trainer and rider to decide which method is best for the horse, so please be flexible in your approach to training flying changes.

As 17th-century master Antoine de Pluvinel said: 'We shall take

1

2

great care not to annoy the horse and spoil his friendly charm, for it is like the scent of a blossom, once lost it will never return.' It's something to bear in mind.

Preparing for a flying change

To produce correct changes, your horse must be advanced enough in his canter to strike off on either lead anywhere in the arena. This is something you can practise.

Remember what we have covered already in the canter and transition chapters, and you'll be fine. The horse must be well-balanced and in a clear, three-beat canter on both reins. You should also have mastered counter-canter (see page 29).

The art of riding a good change is the same as riding very correct simple changes, with a minimum amount of walk steps in between. This is something you can practise, gradually decreasing the walk steps in between strike-offs.

When you have practised all this, ride round the whole arena in counter canter - a good test of how much balance and collection you have achieved. As we have said, all the more advanced movements need a degree of collection.

Carl rides Maxwel through a flying change from left lead to right, counter-canter to canter. The action of his right leg is clear, as it changes from behind the girth in the left-lead canter (1), to on the girth in the right-lead canter (2 and 3).

When to start

When you start introducing canter changes does not depend
on the age of the horse but the factors described earlier. If
your horse is blessed with an uphill, strong, three-beat canter,
it might be an idea to start changes early in his education if
they come naturally and easily. Beware, sometimes people
who have ridden endlessly in counter canter then find it
difficult to get the horse into change mode.

Common flying change faults

- Quarters swinging
- Late behind or in front
- Slowing down or speeding up of the canter
- Quarters coming up

Aids for flying change

- Before asking for the change the rider should let the horse
know by slightly changing the flexion into the direction of the
new canter lead. Note, this does not mean pulling the horse's
head from one side to the other.

● The rider's new outside leg is placed a little further behind the girth and the new outside rein supports the rider's outside leg.

● The rider's new inside leg will move slightly forward to the girth to engage the new inside hind leg.

● During the last phase of the flying change, the rider gives with the inside rein slightly to allow the new leading leg to stride out and continue the first stride of the new canter lead. This has all got to be co-ordinated in one smooth movement but you have already approached this level of co-ordination in your lateral work. Of course the change should be done without any visible movement of the rider's body. Twisting and leaning sideways will only upset the balance, not help. And remember, a flying change should be calm, in rhythm, straight and forward-going.

Carl and Maxwel demonstrate how to make a flying change just before the wall at the end of a diagonal.

Teaching flying changes

There are various ways of teaching changes and you should take a flexible approach. Here are just a few examples.

1 Counter canter on a 20m circle asking for the change on returning to the wall after X.

2 Canter half a 10m circle then a diagonal back to the track. Ask for the change as you head into the new direction on reaching the track.

3 Place a pole 3–5m before the track on the diagonal. Approach in canter, the horse should change as he hops over.

4 Go large in counter-canter and make your flying change in the corner at the end of a long side.

Carl's horses

Otto

Otto has lovely changes, he did from the start. All he needed to do was relax.

Madonna

She went through a running off stage in her changes. She got very excited, so it was even more important that Carl introduced them at the end of a session when she was well tuned in to work. Carl also made sure he stayed calm himself and rewarded her good attempts, as she obviously found changes fun, which led to good expression later on.

Maxwel

His changes needed to be ridden on lots of long sides when schooling at home, as he tended to swing if ridden on diagonals too often.

Using jumps and poles

If your horse is finding it especially difficult to learn changes, he might find it easier if you attempt it in a field as a jumping exercise, as most horses change their canter lead over fences.

You can take advantage of this in the school by placing a pole on the diagonal about 3-5m before the track (see exercise 3, above). Approach it in canter, on reaching the pole, the horse will anticipate the new direction and offer a flying change. This is an especially good exercise if you haven't ridden changes before. The change is set up for you and the horse, so it will build confidence in both of you.

When to try flying changes

When you start teaching your horse flying changes it is better to do it at the end of a session. All you want is one or two good ones and for the horse to finish on a good note. This is far better than trying early in a session when the horse might be over-fresh, which will lead to an uptight or tense performance. If the horse is well worked-in with plenty of transitions, is light on your aids and off your leg, the whole process will be a lot easier.

PROBLEM SOLVING

Horses often tend to rush off when you start to teach flying changes, caused by loss of balance.

What to do

You must be sure the horse is prepared and balanced before you ask for the change. One way to calm the horse down after a change is to ride a circle, then give and retake the reins. Another is to halt, then canter again.

Depending on the horse's temperament it might be advisable to go back to your simple changes and leave flying changes for a few days. Doing other things the horse finds easy before returning to a new lesson will build his confidence.

The most important thing is to give the horse a pat when he's done well. A little praise goes a long way.

Section three

Putting it all into practice

You don't have to compete in dressage, or compete at all to benefit from down to earth dressage training, but it does provide a good way to measure your progress and it can be fun - honestly!

The key to stress-free competition is preparation, and in Section 3 we'll guide you through choosing a test, preparing and practising, and how to cope on the big day. Ever fancied trying dressage to music? Find out how you do it. Carl also describes the tack and equipment that works for him and his horses at home and at shows.

There are also ideas for planning your dressage year, including how to cope with limited facilities in winter, and some special tips for those of you with tense and spooky horses.

Finally, we know how easy it is to get stuck in a rut when schooling at home alone, so to finish, there are plenty of ideas to give you a bit of inspiration and ensure that you, and your horse, keep improving and enjoying down to earth dressage.

Chapter twelve

Practising your dressage test

Why bother to compete? The answer is simple: everyone can be a champion at home but beating the opposition at an away match is the true test of training and your ability to come up with the goods on the day. Preparation is the key to perfect performance. Once you have the schedule for your chosen competition, sit down and browse through the tests on offer.

Choose the right test

Tests in the same category can vary in degree of difficulty, so you need to read the tests and assess which is the best for your horse at his stage of training. Elementary, for example, can vary from the fairly straightforward post-novice type of test to harder ones requiring some collection and shoulder-in. So do your research.

Compete one level down

Well-known riders are often accused of riding in easier tests than their horse is capable of. What you need to bear in mind is that the horse should ideally be working at a higher level at home than the one he is competing at. The work you show in a test should be secure enough to stand up with confidence to the pressures of a competition situation. You're there to show what you can do, not what you can't.

Know the test inside out

There are all sorts of ways of learning tests. Dutch international Sven Rothenberger can be spotted pacing his test out in the stables, Jennie Loriston-Clarke puts her young pupils through it on foot, and lots of riders use test plans or draw them out on a piece of paper. Find out what works for you; you need to know the test so well that if a friend tests you, you can say immediately what comes after any named movement. Then when you are under pressure you can concentrate on riding, not on where to go next.

People might tell you not to practise the test too much because the horse will learn it and anticipate. There's some truth in that, especially if you do the test in its entirety over and over again but the fact is, you do need to practise.

Carl practises 'give and retake the reins' with Elastic, who stretches his outline, rather than stumbling onto his forehand.

Find the weak links

Start a few weeks before the show. Ride through the test and find out where any potential weak links lie. Then you can take those elements and work on them separately. Drilling is not the object of the exercise but incorporating movements into your general routine of suppling and loosening. If something isn't quite working, find out why rather than pressing on and getting tense. For example, if your horse gets tense in walk-to-canter transitions at A, do them somewhere else, do some on a circle and intersperse some trot-canter-trot.

Helping your horse to perform well

When you feel secure with the different elements of the test, ride it through as a whole again. You should feel a significant, confidence-boosting improvement but there will still be bits you are not happy with. That's a symptom of dressage life.

What you need to work out now is how you as a rider can help the horse at these moments. Here are a couple of examples.

● If your horse tends to try and hollow through a transition on the rein he's less supple on, make a note to ride him a little deeper and rounder into the transition.

● If he tends to run in one set of lengthened strides, make a note to pay particular attention to getting him balanced and a little more collected in the corner beforehand, and to getting him straight on the diagonal before you ask him to lengthen.

Video diaries

It's also useful to get someone to video you rehearsing so you can see where improvements could be made and where you could be more accurate. Sometimes when you see it for yourself, it clicks, regardless of how many times your instructor has told you.

Give and re-take the reins

Performing things like 'give and retake the reins' are much easier when you understand what the judge wants to see and you have perfected it at home. It's not a ruse to give the judge a laugh as your horse falls flat on his face or carts you off towards the trade stands. Give and retake is there to prove that you aren't holding the horse in a shape with a vice-like grip and that he is in balance.

Usually give and retake the reins is asked for across a diagonal, so that you can't cheat and keep hold of the outside rein! A quick dash and grab isn't the object of the exercise. If the horse snatches, hollows, or buries his head between his knees, you (and the judge) can safely assume he was too reliant on your hand, albeit for different reasons.

Here's what you need to do for 'give and re-take the reins'

● Make sure the horse is in front of your leg and soft in the contact before you give, which means preparing in the corner beforehand.
● Get the horse straight onto the diagonal; give him a half-halt to make sure he is with you and so are his hind legs.
● Making him a little deeper than normal as you approach X is a good safety catch.
● When you're ready, push your hands up the horse's neck so the reins are loose. For a really slick impression, leave them there for three strides, with the middle stride bang on X.

Salute - and smile

Novice riders often forget to practise their salute but like any situation that is new to the horse, it is best to see how he is going to react. Dressage is all about presentation, so if you haven't practised, you could get to the end of your super first test to find your whip is in the wrong hand, requiring an inelegant shuffle of reins and accoutrements.

● Salute with your right hand, with your whip in the left.
● Men should remove their hats, unless done up with
a safety harness, in which case they can copy the ladies.
There is a danger in whisking your hat off with such a
flourish that the inside of your hat ends up outstretched to
the judge as if you are expecting a large tip for your
fabulous performance!

As you remove your hat, keep the back of your hand and
the back of your hat facing forwards and lower your arm to
slightly behind your upper body, then you won't be
embarrassed if no donation is forthcoming. Keep sitting up,
square, don't unwittingly shift your weight or the horse will
shift out of his lovely square halt. Then just bob your head,
ie drop your chin respectfully to the judge, a full-blown bow
isn't required. Putting your hat back on in a slick movement
needs dexterity acquired by practice, a well fitting hat and
decent haircut.
● Fortunately, ladies don't have to worry about removing
anything. Drop your right arm with the back of your hand
facing forwards as described above, outstretched arms and
palms can look a bit operatic. Again, the smart bob-head-
only-approach applies.
● The main thing about saluting is to look confident and
practise your smile. It might be dressage but it is supposed
to be fun.

Dress rehearsals

Comfortable competition clothes
It'll feel quite alien at the show if you don your new, shiny
top boots, breeches, jacket and hat when you are more
accustomed to riding in jeans and chaps at home. So if you
haven't been to a competition for a while it's a good idea to
have a dress rehearsal rather than giving yourself
something else to panic about on the day. The 'first tail
coat' stage is a classic time for a dress rehearsal as
ticklish tails have often been the cause of a hearty buck in
the ring.

The right tack
If the horse is used to wearing a fluffy numnah at home and
you suddenly plonk his saddle on a smart, streamlined but
thin one at a show, he's going to feel the difference. In
principle it's nice to have special show gear, but on the day
it's a lot easier and cheaper to deal with tack you and your
horse are familiar with. You'll also know which holes
everything goes on.

Arena size and surface
If you can mark out the arena size you'll be competing in
(20 x 40m, or 20 x 60m), it is a good idea to practise

within these confines and ride the movements from marker to marker. Competition arenas often feel surprisingly small once you are in there and the simplest of movements seem to come up faster than you expect.

If you're lucky enough to have a surface to work on, bear in mind that things can feel totally different on grass, so it's wise to have a trial run if your test is on grass. If you work on grass at home but your test is on a surface, you're laughing.

The day before

The day before the test, lay off. Work on suppling, loosening and athletic exercises, not test movements. Getting into a panic at the last minute will only upset you, and the horse will remember it the next day.

You want to head off for the competition with a good feeling and return having given your horse a good experience. There are always going to be things that could be better. But don't forget that even Olympic medals are never won on 100 per cent scores - scores just over 80% suffice for gold!

Break the test down and work on separate elements - here's Carl practising a serpentine with Elastic.

Chapter thirteen

Dressage to music

Riding dressage to music and performing a test that suits your horse is fun and a great confidence booster. Many people don't try freestyle because they don't know how to start and think it will cost a lot. But you can make a freestyle programme without incurring an overdraft.

The first dressage to music programme Carl made was for Legal Democrat's Intermediaire I freestyle at his first international show at Wembley. It was done quickly. In fact Carl decided on it in between classes, which isn't recommended but worked at the time. He came second.

Carl had tribal drum music in mind before he created the programme, liking the heavy, on-the-footfall beat, and it worked very well with Legal Democrat's powerful, rhythmical stride. Unless you are sure of your horse's rhythm and tempo, it might be advisable to start off with a less emphatic beat.

With the music for the Wembley freestyle, during a Christmas shopping expedition, we just happened to walk past a shop and hear it playing. Two minutes and £3.99 later, there was the basis of what was to be a winning programme.

Make a video

The first thing to do is to get someone to video you and your horse in walk, trot and canter, later you'll play that alongside your musical choices.

Choose the music

You don't need to spend a fortune making a tape but you must be willing to put the time into it. That starts with shopping around. Ideally you want to look for instrumental music, no words. In most reputable music shops you can listen to a few tracks before you buy, so take a few CDs into a headphone booth and get a feel for what you like. Do get CDs if you can because of the superior sound quality.

The cheap and cheerful CDs for £2.99 that you can find in supermarkets can be little gems, and at that price you can buy a handful to try out. When you get home, set up a CD player next to the TV and play your musical medley next to your video of the horse's paces, then you can pick pieces that complement his style.

Constructing a test

Choose the best pace

Your freestyle test sheet gives a list of compulsory movements which must be included - for example a novice test will require medium and free walk, working trot including a 15m circle and lengthened strides, working canter including a 20m circle, and halts at the beginning and end.

The most important thing to keep in mind while making the programme is highlighting your horse's best paces. Freestyle also provides a perfect opportunity to hide his weak points. So, for example, if your horse's walk is not that great, walk down the centre line towards the judge rather than doing a 20m circle between E and B, which would give the judge a full view of tense little steps.

Use natural breaks

Lots of people will tell you to make the music fit the test but if you are in a DIY situation you won't have enough technical equipment at your disposal to do this. However, do try to avoid breaking the music in the middle of a phrase. Look for a natural break rather than switching from trot to canter music abruptly.

Fitting music to paces

When you run the music next to the video, you'll see whether the bits you had in mind actually fit your horse's paces. Select your walk, trot and canter themes from the music that illustrates the paces best. Then you have to make sure you fit in all the required movements in that test, and don't be tempted to add things that are not required, which may go wrong and won't earn you any marks. Walk is the most boring bit, so plan to do the minimum in walk and the rest of the movements in trot and canter.

Making your tape

Record your music onto tape. Apart from major internationals most shows will be geared to using tapes rather than CDs. Without chopping into the middle of bars, try and extract the segments of music you are going to use for each pace.

Tests are always timed, from the moment you move off from the first halt until your final halt. So if it says, for example, between four and four-and-a-half minutes, you want to aim for somewhere in the middle.

If you allow, say, half a minute for walk, the four remaining minutes should be split between trot and canter according to which is your horse's best pace. If it's trot, look at spending two-and-a-half minutes in trot and one and a half in canter, and vice versa if your canter is more impressive. Concentrate on the best pace.

Once you've got a basic idea, you need to refine it, by going through each piece of music, finding suitable breaks and timing the various sections using a stopwatch. Putting the pieces together onto a tape takes precision, so if you can get a friend to help as tape operator while you do the stopping and starting, it'll be much easier.

Your start and finish

For entrance music, try to take the end of a piece of music, which is often the most dramatic bit. Allow approximately five to 10 seconds, depending on whether your horse likes standing still or not, to perform a decent halt, salute and put your hands back on the reins again. You also want to go out with a bang, so try and use an end piece here too, then you won't have to cut the music and you'll achieve a natural finish.

Matching test to tape

Having got your tape together, you have to put the test to it. Take your tape player to the school or borrow a Walkman and ride to the music.

Use the arena

As it is a freestyle, it doesn't matter if the trot music stops half way round a 20m circle, it is up to you where you change direction, you don't have to use the letters at all. But do make the test use the whole arena. Also, you don't have to stick to traditional markers. Use three-quarter lines, loops, short diagonals, half circles and so on to make a more innovative ground pattern.

Make the most of your horse

The thing about freestyle is that it is great fun. It brings out your horse's personality as well as your own. Needless to say, if you have a light, elegant horse, you won't be illustrating his personality by riding to the music of an oompah band. Likewise, if you've got a big, powerful horse, music from Swan Lake is liable to raise a few chuckles from spectators.

If your horse is a big mover, use big circles and diagonals. If he is more the neat, tidy type, use a few more twiddly bits such as smaller circles and loops. As we've said, freestyle is all about capitalising on your assets.

Monitoring your progress

Get someone to video your new freestyle. Then you can see how the ground pattern looks and that you are making best use of the phrasing in the music. For example, a crescendo illustrates lengthening, so that's a good time to ride your lengthened strides.

Professional production

Of course, if you haven't got time, there are plenty of specialist producers who will put together a music tape if you send them a video of your test. Bear in mind however, that unless you discuss it thoroughly beforehand, it may not be your personal taste in music.

Before the Olympics in Atlanta, medal winner Isabell Werth rode to a special recording, *Gigolo's Journey* and Anky van Grunsven's music, *Bonfire's Symphony*, was specially composed by a Dutch duo famous for TV commercials. It was recorded by a 200-piece orchestra and was available on CD after the event. But not all freestyle productions have to be quite so ambitious!

Take your time

Freestyle need not be expensive at all. As we have said, Carl's Wembley tape cost under a tenner, but it does take time and patience. Expect to spend some money the first few times but then you'll end up with a supply of ideas and a library of CDs suitable for freestyle.

Allow several days at least to do your production. It's not worth the stress of trying to do it all the night before your test, especially as freestyle should look fluent, accomplished and stylish, whatever the level.

Carl and Legal Democrat are experienced and successful dressage to music competitors - they love the opportunity to show off!

On the day

● Have two tapes with you so you have got a spare. Things do go wrong with equipment and you don't want to end up with all your hard work wasted as your precious tape is irretrievably devoured by the organiser's tape deck.
● Equipment varies, so if you find the tape running slower or faster than you expected, don't panic. Try and stay in control and relaxed, concentrating on the rhythm - your horse will generally follow you.
● If you end up slightly ahead or short of where you expected to be, remember a freestyle doesn't have to be on the official markers, you can cut a corner or put in an extra circle. If you have practised enough and are really familiar with your music, you'll be more ready to adapt if necessary.
● Relax and enjoy yourself.

Chapter fourteen

Working through the seasons

Planning your year is an important part of achieving your goals. Carl spends the winter concentrating on bringing on the younger horses and does most of his competitive campaigning during the summer. The traditional competition season is still spring and summer, when the road to the championships opens with qualifiers. A bit of forward planning will make the most of your summer campaign.

There is plenty to do in the winter as well, you don't need to give up your training during less fair weather times of the year. In fact you might find good opportunities to consolidate your work so far and even try moving up a level when there's less pressure than during the summer.

Winter work

If you have an indoor school, or an outdoor school with a good surface, or a well-drained field, you can continue improving your dressage quite easily.

Just remember that as you wouldn't relish a run in the pouring rain, neither will your horse be able to put his full concentration into travers with the rain dripping down his ears. Be fair in your expectations. Even if you haven't got a decent surface to work on, you can still keep ticking over nicely.

Constructive roadwork

Even if you are reduced to road work when the field is muddy, you can still work on keeping the horse straight and attentive. Just remember not to shorten the horse from the front end or your winter's work will have been a spoiled walk.

Self-improvement

Watch out for courses and schooling days in your area. Riding clubs often hire an indoor school for a day where you can join in group instruction or a special interest day on test riding, for example. There are also plenty of lecture demonstrations throughout the winter. Go and watch a well-known rider or trainer for a bit of inspiration.

Working on Maxwel's half-pass; winter is a good time to brush up your technique.

If the weather is really dire, consult the travel brochures. Seriously, it might be an idea to think about booking your horse in for a couple of weeks with a trainer to bring him on a bit while you take some lessons. Suggest it as your next Christmas present!

Winter holidays

Making the decision to give your horse a winter break will depend on how much he has done during the summer season. Carl's older horses have a couple of weeks when they're turned out daily in the field and brought in at night. The younger ones have their breaks during the summer season, while Carl is busy with the experienced campaigners, and are ready to get back to school in autumn.

If you really need a break and want to turn your horse away completely in winter, remember it takes far longer to bring an older horse's muscles back to fitness and suppleness than those of a young horse. Riders who just have one horse to keep them in trim should consider this aspect as well! You can give your horse an easy time but still keep him interested by alternating light riding or hacking and turning out on different days - it doesn't have to be all or nothing.

Competing in winter

There is a whole range of dressage competitions on offer through the winter months nowadays.

Move on up

Apart from novice and elementary, venues with qualifiers for winter medium often run a non-qualifier as well or even an advanced medium, so this is your chance to try a more challenging test. The atmosphere of winter shows is often less pressurised and you'll find there are others having a go. Just remember, don't think about trying a new level until you have done your homework and are really prepared.

One major advantage of winter competition is access to an indoor school. If you are going to use a show as an opportunity for a proper work-out on a surface, go for the familiar not

If all else fails

When it is really frozen of course, all you can do is tuck your horse up with a hay net, settle yourself down with a video of the world championships, and dream.

the new. It's also worth remembering your prime reason for entering before you head off and complain to the secretary about the boggy warm-up area.

Warming up

If the warm-up area isn't good, you'll just have to adapt. If the outside track is dry, work in a good forward rising trot and where you can, add transitions to get the horse more attentive and working from behind while keeping an eye out to avoid collision with other riders. You can use a little bend to the outside and some shoulder-in to get him listening even if you have to give up the idea of circles through the lake in the middle.

If the venue is close by, you can always ride in a bit at home first. Especially with youngsters on their first few outings, it means you get the fun and games over and there is less of the fire-breathing dragon act when you arrive at the show to find a warm-up area the size of a postage stamp.

Entering the school

When it is your turn to go in, especially if your horse is not used to working indoors, be aware that he is going to take a look around and will feel a bit insecure as the door shuts behind him and he's separated from his friends. Be there for him, give him a reassuring pat and get moving. Lengthen him in trot or canter down the long side and shorten him before the corner ready to shoulder-in (a good spook-busting tip) past the judge's car at the top end as you work round before the test.

Boards and walls

In a big school, the white boards set out to mark the arena can also turn out to be a source of horror. Be prepared to use more leg, but don't be fooled into clamping up and losing it by using too much hand. If the school is arena sized, the walls will help you, but the corners will help you more if you use them properly to half-halt and prepare the horse for what is coming up.

Avoiding chills

Before and after the test, your priority is to keep your horse warm, use a rug while you are warming up and put it back on to walk round afterwards. The quickest way to give a horse a chill is to plonk him, still blowing, in the lorry or trailer, while you go and have a nice cup of tea.

Be prepared

If you are using a lower level test as an exercise but training more advanced movements at home, don't be surprised if your horse, like a kid coming out with a precocious word at an embarrassing moment, pops in something he thinks you want, but isn't in the test. If he does, you should have ensured he was listening more, it's not his fault and don't punish him for showing off.

In fact flexibility could be the motto for winter work, if you think constructively and don't get frustrated by what you can't do. You can have a lot of fun learning new things with your horse, but keep in mind that it should be fun for him too.

Competing in summer

If you have a goal in sight such as reaching the area finals or even the national championships, it pays to start early. It will be less pressurised, as if it doesn't come off first time, you've a few more chances to qualify, and as popular summer shows can be over-subscribed, you have more time to re-plan if you are unlucky enough to be balloted out.

Hot days

We all hope for hot days during the summer, but if one of those elusive events occurs on a competition day rather than a lie-in-the-garden day off, you might have to adapt your normal schedule. This applies at home as well as at competitions; if you are wilting in the heat, it is more than likely that your horse will be too. Shorten your warm-up time accordingly. If you are not sure what the reaction will be, it is worth getting the horse out for two short warming up periods. In between, you can give him a refreshing wipe over.

Keep cool

After the test, give the horse a cooling wash, then walk him round. Be aware that your lorry or trailer might get very hot, so maximise ventilation. Offer the horse lots of opportunities for drinks. Even if he doesn't drink, spongeing his mouth with a clean sponge and fresh water will perk him up.

Fly away

Don't forget the fly spray! Apply it before during the tacking up process, and if you've got a helper, an additional quick wipe over before your test usually pays off. Use a spray-soaked cloth, not a potentially alarming spray just before a test.

Hard ground

So many competitions are on proper dressage surfaces now, but even at a big show, you may find your test is on a surface, but your warm up is on grass. If it's hard, warm up in the effective but not intensive way described above. Going for your maximum extensions on hard ground could put your horse out for the rest of the season if you jar his joints up.

Cool warm-ups

Work effectively, rather than intensively. Your transition training, some trot-halt-rein back-trot work to get the horse working from behind can take the place of lots of medium and extended work. Give the horse lots of breaks and perhaps some leg-yield in walk to keep him listening.

Keep an eye on how the class is running, if there is any delay. You don't want the horse 'cooked' by the time you go into the arena.

Chapter fifteen

Tense, spooky and excitable horses

Some horses are tense and spooky by nature but that does not mean they are useless. Very often, these are the horses that develop into better performers than the quiet, laid-back types. Carl believes that if you can tame a hot horse, you'll end up with a good horse. Here are some of his tension-busting ideas.

● Tension can be created not only by the horse but also by the rider. If you are a nervous rider, it is not a good idea to be in partnership with a tense horse - both of you need security. This pairing could be a time-bomb.

● The purpose of the exercise and the sense of achievement when riding a tense, nervous or spooky horse is not in squashing the horse's personality, but in getting the horse to work on-side with you, the rider.

Tackling tension

There are many ways of tackling tension problems. Some or all of these may work for you and your horse.

Check him out

Firstly, do check thoroughly that the horse is not in any pain or discomfort from tack or physical problems.

Understand the problem

Once you have established that there are no physical problems, try to understand your horse's physical reasons for tension. Tension often manifests itself in the neck.

What to do

Carl finds that some horses can be ridden through tension to relaxation by riding the head and neck deeper and rounder.

Madonna looks rather tense and anxious - she'd probably rather run on than lengthen properly in trot.

Turn him out

Obviously one of the simplest methods of helping the tense, buzzy horse to relax is to turn him out on a regular basis. This is a great form of relaxation.

Little and often

When you ride a horse who has a tendency to be tense, either running away from you, or stiff in the neck and back, producing short, choppy strides, you can't solve the problem by riding him for hours and hours. In Carl's experience, this creates a vicious circle.

What to do
It is far better to ride the horse two or three times a day for 20 minutes at a time. The idea is not to wear the horse out but to give him a greater understanding of what you want and build up his confidence.

Take a contact

People are often frightened to touch a tense horse's mouth. Saying your horse will calm down when he is tired of charging around misses the point. An out of control horse is a nervous horse.

What to do
The problem can be solved by the rider taking a contact with the reins and the legs, so that the horse obtains confidence more or less straight away. By stretching the horse and letting him know you are there, you can often transform a tense horse into a happy one in a short time.

Go down a gear

In general, tense, spooky horses tend to be very forward-going. You don't want to discourage this desire to go forwards but, as we've said, it's a fruitless task to keep bashing on at top speed hoping it will calm the horse down.

What to do

Take it back a gear and work on exercises, such as plenty of small circles in walk, plenty of slow transitions, and moving the horse in and out away from your leg on circles. All these exercises are designed to make the horse more accepting of the rider. Once you have achieved softness the horse is letting go, which basically means the horse hands himself over to the rider so then you can really start to ride the horse forwards again.

Dos and don'ts

What can you do when a horse spooks at something that frightens him, like a plastic bag, a tractor or even the rails around the dressage arena?

DON'T ram your legs on and force the horse to look at whatever it is he doesn't like, then let him run past at 100 miles an hour - again, your control is lost.

DO keep returning to the simple pace of walk, which gives the horse time to focus on whatever he is passing.

DON'T ride strongly, hanging on to the mouth for grim death, which always seems to make the horse spook more.

DO play with the rein so the horse does not feel trapped.

Dealing with excitable horses

Excitability is usually a rather different situation, caused by a strange atmosphere or lots going on, rather than nervousness or tension, though it can be a combination of factors. Here's the best way to deal with horses who get excitable at shows.

● Arrive at a show in plenty of time to allow the horse the chance to see his new surroundings.

● Take the horse out when you arrive and work him calmly, with stretching, bending and general relaxation exercises, rather than movements, before you start thinking about your test and nerves or stress kick in.

● Then return to the lorry and put the horse away in a relaxed way so that he can digest what he has done.

● Bring him out again 20 to 30 minutes before the test. This achieves a much better result than riding the horse for two hours, and trying to force him into a submissive attitude.

Is he excitable or nervous?

You need to be able to differentiate whether the horse is excitable for a good reason, or has learnt through previous experience that this behaviour means he can escape work. If it's the latter, you may feel you want to 'bottom him out', which may entail carrying on working him until you achieve

Remember, the horse must learn to control his energy, not do without it.

Carl encourages Madonna to relax by riding her deep and round; working on a circle can also help.

what you want. However, this is something better dealt with by an expert trainer. Always look for alternative ways.

Never despair

In previous chapters we have described what to do with horses who jog in walk or run in trot and canter. These are all symptoms of tension in one form or another, or a form of lack of submission but they can be dealt with, so please don't despair.

Think of one of the best dressage horses of all time, Rembrandt. He was always excited, he spooked and still does in his retirement years. Many people would have given up and deemed the horse too difficult and bolshy, but through clever, thoughtful, sympathetic riding and relaxation techniques, Nicole Uphoff was able to produce some of the most magnificent dressage displays ever seen. At top level, dressage looks best when it is a combination of controlled power and energy, almost verging on tension at times.

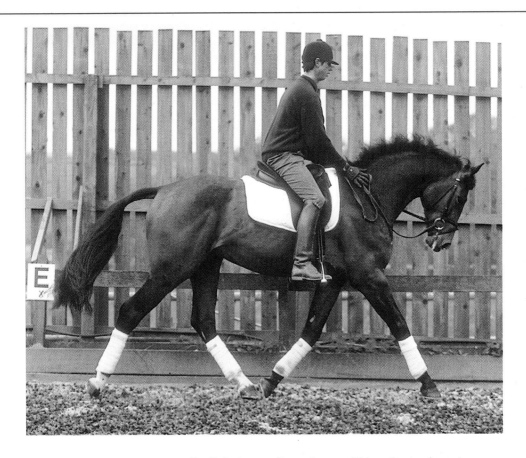

Don't feel, even if your horse still has the tendency to spookiness and tension at the grand old age of seven or eight, that it is too late to find ways round it. You can channel tension to work for you, not against you.

Tension-busting tips

● Ideally you should warm up in walk for about 10 minutes before you start schooling but if the horse is particularly tense, move into trot and settle him rather than insisting on a calm walk, and failing to get it.
● Sitting trot can make the rider tense. You don't have to sit all the time when you're schooling or sit the whole way through prelim and novice tests. Go rising rather than creating tension in yourself and the horse.
● To reduce the likelihood of tension during schooling, give the horse plenty of breaks. Give him a pat, let him stretch down and forward.
● Preparation reduces tension. Don't surprise the horse with sudden sharp turns or transitions, half-halt a few steps before to warn him. Prepare for a test by learning it really well beforehand, so you can relax and concentrate on riding when you get there. Do a slightly easier test than you are capable of this - will boost your confidence and help you relax.

Reward good behaviour with a pat and some encouragement - nervous horses need particularly confident and reassuring riders.

Chapter sixteen

Tack

T he most important thing when it comes to choosing tack for schooling is comfort for you and the horse. Here's what Carl finds works best for him - but don't worry about the bank manager yet, these are guidelines, not rules cast in stone.

Getting started

From the very start with his young horses, Carl likes to use a jointed synthetic loose ring snaffle bit. Horses are born with sensitive mouths, although not all end up with them. The idea is to preserve their sensitivity. Youngsters seem very happy to start learning to take the contact in the synthetic bit, and Carl has not yet found a horse that doesn't like the flexibility of the jointed snaffle.

The noseband is just as important as the bit and of course works in conjunction with it. It's sometimes hard to know how tight the noseband should be, but Carl warns against using a tight drop or flash noseband on a baby horse.

With the young horse that opens his mouth a lot and fiddles too much, it may seem like an easy option, but the last thing you want to do is clamp his mouth shut at such an early stage with a tight noseband. If you do that, he'll never learn to relax his jaw.

Later on perhaps, if the problem is ongoing, then a flash or drop noseband can be very useful. Otto for example, being an opinionated stallion, eventually needed a reminder to concentrate and not keep munching and talking all the way through class.

Carl also has a trusty synthetic saddle that is used on all youngsters when they're first backed. It is very light and resilient, which it needs to be with some youngsters and has an over-strap on the flaps to keep them flat. It's amazing what it has been through!

Sometimes a drop noseband - not too tightly fitted - is useful with a youngster such as Elastic.

A jointed snaffle with synthetic mouthpiece - Carl starts youngsters in bits like this to preserve the sensitivity of their mouths (above).

Bits

The type of bit you should use, how thick or thin it should be, can only be gauged by the feel the horse gives to your hand, once you have established that it fits the horse properly.

Bit tips

● Barring problems, a bit that fits well should cause just a nice little wrinkle on either side of the mouth.
● With a gelding, it is a good idea to have the bit slightly higher to avoid the tushes (small teeth that may grow between the incisors and molars).
● If the horse has a tendency to be hollow, it is better to have the bit slightly lower so it has more effect on the bars of the mouth.
● With horses that tend to drop the contact and go behind the bit, it is better to have the bit one hole higher than normal.
● As he puts their bridles on, Carl always gives his horses a couple of pieces of sugar to help them to taste the bit and start to salivate.

A loose-ringed snaffle in German silver with a 'lozenge', Carl uses mild, comfortable bits like this for everyday schooling (below).

Carl's choice

For general, everyday work Carl uses bits made of German silver, a special alloy containing copper that encourages salivation. He likes loose-ring snaffles with a nugget shaped link in the middle. These bits seem to have more play and feel in the reins than fixed ring bits.

Double bridles

When to start

Double bridles give you the ability to fine tune your horse's work much more than a snaffle, though of course they require more refined riding. So, when should you introduce one?

Carl stresses that it's most important to be very sure that your horse is accepting the snaffle happily, willingly and with a good contact. Any horse that has mouth or contact problems is not ready for a double bridle.

When his horses are happy in their snaffles, Carl likes to introduce a double bridle fairly soon, his horses tend to reach higher levels quite quickly, and he likes them to be well prepared and comfortable in their mouths.

It might seem a little controversial to introduce the double bridle by the time his horses are five or six years old but this is simply because by the time they are six or seven, hopefully they will be competing at a level where a double bridle must be worn, and Carl likes them to be thoroughly accustomed to the double for enough time to develop confidence and be happy in it.

Of course, you don't need to introduce a double bridle to your horse at any specific age. Snaffles are compulsory in preliminary and novice dressage classes. From elementary level to advanced medium you have the choice of using a snaffle or a double, (although you shouldn't be looking at riding elementary in a double), but from advanced and above, a double bridle is compulsory.

Fitting tips

- Any bridle must be well-fitted, but this is especially important with the double bridle.
- Fit the bridoon one hole higher than with your normal snaffle, as this gives more room for the curb to lie kindly in the mouth.

Curb chain checkpoints

The curb chain should be fitted so that it comes into action when the cheeks of the curb bit form a 45 degree angle to the vertical. Carl cautions that there is nothing worse than when a curb chain is too loose and the shanks of the curb have to be pulled horizontal to the ground to bring it into action. It not only looks awful, but means the bit is not working properly and could be doing damage.

Carl cautions that curb chains, and bits, must be treated with great care. The curb chain can be a severe piece of equipment and must be used carefully, as it lies in a very sensitive part of the horse's anatomy which, we're reliably told, is also an acupuncture point. This is why horses tend to drop their heads more readily with a double on.

However, the curb should never be used as the rider's way of bringing the horse onto the bit. The snaffle rein must be the dominant rein, the curb is merely a refinement of the aids.

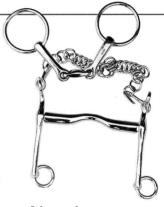

A loose-ring narrow bridoon with a 'lozenge' and a shallow-ported Weymouth - Carl uses bits like this when he introduces a horse to a double bridle (above).

A straight-cut dressage saddle is purpose-built for the job (below left).

Carl's horses

As a general rule, Carl uses a loose-ring, narrow bridoon with a 'lozenge' in the middle, and a standard Weymouth with a low port, again, they are usually in German silver.

There are exceptions, of course, and he stresses that it may take some experimentation to find absolutely the right combination of bits for an individual horse. For example, it wasn't easy to find a curb that Otto was happy with. After many attempts at finding a suitable curb bit, he settled on a narrow, straight-bar Weymouth, as the less metal Otto has in his mouth, the happier he is.

Fantastic Elastic got his double bridle at the start of his sixth year. Again, Carl was careful to find a suitable curb. Elastic has a sensitive mouth so he has a Weymouth type known as a forward port. As the port comes forward when you take a contact, not upwards on the tongue, there is much less pressure on the horse's mouth.

How to introduce a double bridle

Carl finds it helpful to hack the horse in the new bridle so he can relax and savour the new feeling without pressure. After two or three weeks of this laid-back introduction, he'll be ready for schooling in a double bridle.

Reins

Carl's preference is for a webbing (continental) snaffle rein and a leather curb rein.

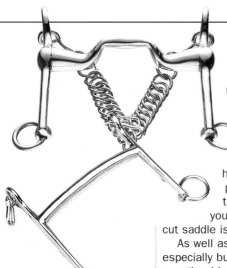

Saddles

As a professional who spends hours in the saddle, when Carl feels his young horses have reached a stage of maturity where their shape is fairly established, they have their own dressage saddles made. But let's get one thing straight: a dressage saddle is not essential for successful schooling.

If your main interest is jumping - or hacking, or endurance - a well-fitting general purpose will see you through everyday work and the occasional foray to a dressage competition. If you are a dressage enthusiast, however, a straighter-cut saddle is the purpose-designed tool for the job.

As well as being tailored to each horse, Carl's saddles are especially built to suit his own physique. The saddle must fit you, the rider, and be comfortable for you, as well comfortable for the horse.

Carl's saddles are especially cut to accommodate his enviably long legs. Even if you can't afford a tailor-made saddle, it is worth bearing in mind that different saddles can help with different problems – if your leg comes too far forward or back; the depth of seat and how close you like to feel to the horse; if your horse has a tendency to saddle sores – all these elements should be taken into account when choosing a saddle.

For the dressage horse, it is important that the saddle should sit well behind the shoulder, so it does not obscure the shoulder and affect its free movement - this also helps the horse carry the weight further back. All the rules that apply to other saddles should also be applied to fitting a dressage saddle, you just have extra specialist considerations to take into account.

Good equipment does not come cheap, but it is always worth investing in professional opinion for bit and saddle fittings. You pay for quality, and quality will always pay for itself in the end.

Carl uses a Weymouth with forward-facing port like this for Elastic, who has a sensitive mouth (top).

Otto doesn't like too much metal in his mouth, so Carl rides him in a narrow, straight-bar Weymouth like this (above).

Madonna in her 'grown up' tack: double bridle, dressage saddle, white numnah and leg bandages

Chapter seventeen

Keep on Improving

If you've followed the advice in this book avidly, you and your horse will be able to put together all the ingredients of an advanced medium or an international three-day event dressage test. So you should be able to go out and win one, right? No, realistically, if you have achieved a good basic level in your training, you and your horse should have touched on all these ingredients but you will be some way off from performing them at markers, on command, in a slick fashion. So where do you go from here?

Listen to the horse

To produce his best work in a competition atmosphere, in unfamiliar surroundings, any horse needs to be secure and confident at the level he is competing at.

If an exercise is not as near perfect as you can get it at home, you're not going to get it in a test. Remember this when you see professional riders working in at shows and exhibiting a few steps of work far more advanced than they'll be producing in the test. Contrary to comments you often hear at the ringside, they are not pot-hunting. The simple approach is, as with all forms of training, to take your time and listen to the horse to see whether he is mature enough physically and mature enough in his mind to absorb new lessons. Then work on new things in combination with all the work the horse is already confident in.

If, at this stage, you've achieved a good shoulder-in, a promising half-pass and a good change in canter either way, even if it takes a few goes to get it right, you are doing well. So, how are you going to make further progress? By going back to basics and revising. Here are some guidelines.

Ask yourself:

● Is my horse working in a good forward rhythm, in balance in walk, trot and canter, and does he react immediately to my leg?
● Is he keeping the correct sequence, particularly in walk and canter?
● Is he even and light in the contact?
● Is he straight on straight lines, and bending equally on turns and laterally?
● Is he maintaining his balance and carriage in transitions?
● Am I sitting with a secure, soft seat and able to give the horse signals he understands?

Carl schools a very young horse like Brad for only about 20 minutes, five days a week.

If you can't answer 'yes' to all the questions, you need to revise. If you can, well done, but there is always room for improvement. If you feel you have a good basis but haven't had the courage to try the more advanced work in the last few pages, now is your chance - you can do it.

The rider

When training your horse, it is just as important that you pay attention to your own style and performance. The horse is only going to understand what you want if you put it to him in a clear way. Having said that, Carl doesn't expect his pupils, or himself, to sit pretty at the expense of taking action. If you want something you have to ask for it but constant revision of your own position is going to help your horse and your progress in the long term. If you don't have a regular trainer, there are still lots of ways you can help yourself.

Video view

If you can, engage the help of a friend with a video camera who is willing to film you as you ride. When you watch it later, concentrate on all the faults you have picked up and try and figure out why they are happening.
● If, for example, you are collapsing to the outside in lateral work, practise sitting into the direction you are travelling by pushing more weight into the inside heel and looking where you are heading.
● Check that you are not bringing your outside heel up as you ask the horse to move away from your leg.
● If you can spot any general stiffness in your own position, deal with it as you would with your horse. Does it hurt anywhere? Get it checked out. If there is no injury, embark on a programme of suppling exercises for yourself.

The horse

Check to make sure that your horse is really going forwards, in balance, at all times.

Work without stirrups

If you want to work without stirrups, to settle into the horse more and lengthen and relax your leg, do it when you and the horse are worked-in and have an established rhythm, that way you'll get maximum benefit.

On the lunge

If you really trust your friend, get him or her to lunge you for a short time, just to give you a chance to focus on what you are doing as the horse makes a transition, as he bends through a circle and so on. It doesn't have to be equestrian gymnastics to make a difference.

Forwards

You can only say your horse is really going forwards if he reacts off your leg aid straight away and maintains his forward momentum without nagging from you. The habit of nagging is also a major cause of the horse being behind the leg. Don't nag, act. If the horse does not respond first time to your leg, halt, give him one swift kick and as he reacts, let him go, don't stop him with your hands.

If he gallops off, that's great, you've got your reaction and as you let him go, he knows exactly what you mean. Then next time you ask him to go, he knows to go NOW, not in 10 seconds time, and he knows you'll allow him to do it.

Then the more the horse learns to react, the more you can lighten your aid.

Keeping a good contact

If there is anything going awry here, look at yourself first. Are your allowing with your hand in upward and downward transitions, on the inside or outside rein in shoulder-in and on turns? Remember, in a bend, once the inside rein has indicated the degree of bend, you should be ready to ease the hand if you want to avoid tilting, resistance or stiffness. If the contact problem really isn't down to you (and do be honest)

Carl lets Madonna stretch down and gives her a pat - frequent rewards are vital when you're training a horse.

Warm up and cool down

Remember to warm up and cool off at each end of a schooling session. Carl's horses all walk at the beginning and end of their work. They walk in the school before they start work for 10 minutes or so, rugs on in cold weather, and at the end it is usually a couple of turns round the field on a loose rein so they are always allowed a chance to relax and step out.

remedy the situation with lots of transitions, on and back, and encouraging a slightly deeper outline.

Balance

To maintain and ensure balance, the half-halt is your tool. Don't let half-halt slip to the back of your mind in favour of coasting. Before every transition you make, before corners, before you ask the horse anything, a half-halt alerts the horse that something is about to happen and gives him that bit of gathering power as the hind legs come further underneath, to carry it out well. Remember also to allow the half-halt through with your hands, you won't engage a new gear when you've still got the brake on.

Remember with horses that rush in their work, transitions are your key to establishing control. Lots of them, on a circle, will help teach the over-eager horse to wait.

Perfect paces

It is essential to keep in mind as you try new lessons that the quality of the gaits is paramount. It might happen that you get some tension as you both try a new lesson. The thing is never to allow it to develop into a situation that may spoil the basic pace. Stop what you are doing and go back to basics. If the horse is tightening, even hollowing, work him forwards on fluent lines in a deeper outline so he can stretch over his top line. Remember the on and back routine already described and ride a few lengthened strides within a gait – then go back to normal. Use lots of transitions to re-establish a soft contact from a relaxed horse that is waiting for your signals.

Not straight in transitions?

● Are you allowing the horse forward, and in canter, are you asking for too much bend?
● Similarly if your straight lines are going wobbly, check your contact, check your energy, make sure the horse is allowed forward.
● With turns and circles, smooth turns need energy. Don't let the momentum drop as you come into the turn and to prepare for the turn with an alerting, balancing half-halt.

And finally...

There is no such thing as a backward step in training, even going back to basics. The world's top grand prix horses don't practise piaffe and passage every day or even every week. Once lessons are learned, the key to producing good work from a happy, enthusiastic horse is to have his body and mind in the best shape. Think gymnastic for your horse's body, confident for his mind, and new lessons will be a joy not a battle. And remember, always reward the horse for every effort - no matter how small.

Now, every time you set out on a schooling session, you have the tools to make it a planned, purposeful one. Remember, training takes time. Like Rome, dressage horses, or simply well-trained horses, aren't made in a day. If something doesn't go right, take a step back and build it up again. Most of all, as we said at the beginning, listen to your horse. It's the best way to get him to listen to you. And finally, having learned the big dressage secret - that there isn't one - good luck and have fun.